W9-CAY-701

THE COMPLETE

Guidebook to Yosemite

NATIONAL PARK

STEVEN P. MEDLEY

WITH UPDATES BY PETER BREWITT

Yosemite Conservancy, Yosemite National Park

For Jane and the boys

....

YOSEMITE
CONSERVANCY.
yosemiteconservancy.org

Yosemite Conservancy's Mission
Providing for Yosemite's future is our passion. We inspire people to support projects and programs that preserve and protect Yosemite National Park's resources and enrich the visitor experience.

Library of Congress Control Number: 2011943068

Caveat
Given the rapidity with which things change, the accuracy and completeness of the contents of this book cannot be guaranteed. The publisher and author assume no legal responsibility for the appreciation or depreciation of the value of any premises, commercial or otherwise, by reason of their inclusion in, or exclusion from this book. Further, the names of businesses mentioned here are provided as a service to readers and not as an endorsement or guarantee.

Cover photograph of Yosemite Falls by Jeff Grandy

Cover /Interior Design: J. Spittler/Jamison Design

Maps by Ben Pease, Pease Press Cartography, based on original maps by Bill Kuhn and the National Park Service

ISBN 978-1-930238-28-2

Printed in China by Everbest Printing Co. through Four Colour Imports, Ltd., Louisville, Kentucky

1 2 3 4 5 6 – 16 15 14 13 12

Contents

Marmot

A view of Half Dome

Acknowledgments

Thanks to everyone who helped in the production of this book, including
Pat Wight, Penny Otwell, Holly Warner, Anne Steed, Laurel Rematore, Beth
Pratt, Mary Vocelka, Ann Gushue, Jim Snyder, Linda Eade, Len McKenzie,
Dean Shenk, Marla LaCass, Laurel Boyers, Craig Bates, N. King Huber, Jan van
Wagtendonk, Peter Browning, Jim Alinder, Bill Neill, Mike Osborne, Mono Lake
Committee, Keith Walklet, Nancy Lusignan, Kris Fister, Bob Jones, Tori Keith,
Delaware North Concessionaire, Jack and Gay Reineck, and Norma Craig.

In the creation of the new edition, the publisher especially thanks Bob Hansen
for his spirit of generosity, knowledgeable suggestions, and expert guidance on
all things Yosemite. Also many thanks are owed to the National Park Service and
its dedicated employees, especially Linda Eade, Mary Kline, Brenna Lissoway, and
Laura Patten.

This new edition was created with funds from the Steve Medley Memorial Fund.
The Steve Medley Memorial Fund supports publications and educational projects
and programs that enhance Yosemite Conservancy's contributions to Yosemite
National Park. If you would like to make a tax-deductible donation to honor
Steve's legacy of excellence in publications and educational projects and pro-
grams, send your gift, designated for the "YC Steve Medley Memorial Fund," to
Yosemite Conservancy at P.O. Box 230, El Portal, CA 95318. You can also donate
online at yosemiteconservancy.org, or by calling 1-800-469-7275.

A dogwood branch over the Merced River

Half Dome at twilight from Glacier Point

1 | Welcome to Yosemite

Yosemite National Park is one of the best places on Earth. Yosemite holds rugged 13,000-foot mountains, two major rivers, living glaciers, and broad alpine meadows. It has the largest (and smallest) trees on earth, the tallest waterfall in North America, and a mountain that looks like it's been cut in half. It is our oldest wilderness park, a mecca for photographers, and the world center of rock climbing. Millions of people visit the park every year, and all of them can find true solitude. If you've come for intense adventures, climbing, skiing, or backpacking, Yosemite is the place for you. If you've come to relax, enjoy the scenery, and take some time out from your life…Yosemite is still the place for you. From the joys of the high country and Tuolumne Meadows in the summer to the gushing waterfalls of the spring to cross-country skiing in the winter, there is no bad time to visit Yosemite National Park.

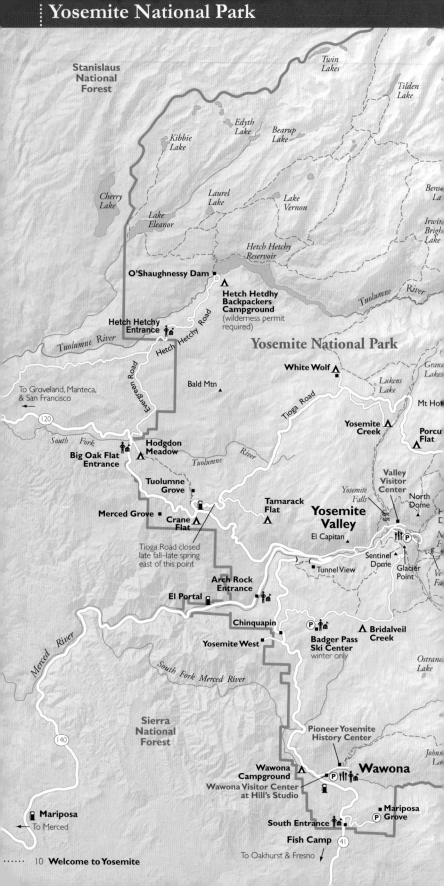

Stanislaus
National
Forest

Twin
Lakes

Tilden
Lake

Kibbie
Lake

Edyth
Lake

Bearup
Lake

Cherry
Lake

Laurel
Lake

Lake
Vernon

Bens
La

Lake
Eleanor

Hetch Hetchy
Reservoir

Tuolumne   River

Irwin
Brigh
Lake

O'Shaughnessy Dam

⛰ **Hetch Hetchy
Backpackers
Campground**
(wilderness permit
required)

Yosemite National Park

Hetch Hetchy
Entrance

Tuolumne   River

White Wolf

Lukens
Lake

Gran
Lakes

Hetch Hetchy Road

Mt Ho

To Groveland, Manteca,
& San Francisco

Bald Mtn

Tioga Road

Evergreen Road

**Yosemite
Creek**

**Porcu
Flat**

120

South   Fork

**Hodgdon
Meadow**

Tuolumne   River

Valley
Visitor
Center

Yosemite
Falls

North
Dome

**Big Oak Flat
Entrance**

**Tuolumne
Grove**

**Tamarack
Flat**

**Yosemite
Valley**

Merced Grove

**Crane
Flat**

Tioga Road closed
late fall–late spring
east of this point

El Capitan

Sentinel
Dome

Glacier
Point

Ve
Fa

**Arch Rock
Entrance**

Tunnel View

El Portal

Chinquapin

⛰ **Bridalveil
Creek**

Ostrana
Lake

Merced   River

Yosemite West

**Badger Pass
Ski Center**
winter only

Sierra
National
Forest

South   Fork   Merced   River

**Pioneer Yosemite
History Center**

140

Wawona

**Wawona
Campground**

**Wawona Visitor Center
at Hill's Studio**

Johns
La

Mariposa
To Merced

**Mariposa
Grove**

South Entrance

Fish Camp

41

To Oakhurst & Fresno

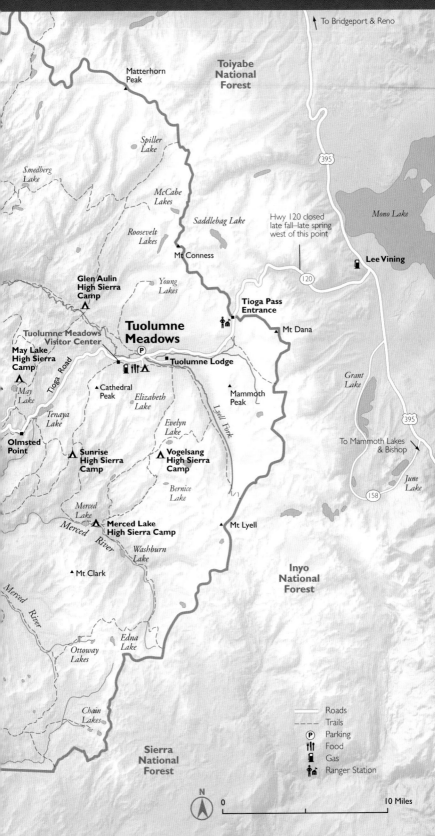

To Bridgeport & Reno

Toiyabe National Forest

Matterhorn Peak

Spiller Lake

Smedberg Lake

McCabe Lakes

Saddlebag Lake

Mono Lake

Roosevelt Lakes

Mt Conness

Hwy 120 closed late fall–late spring west of this point

Lee Vining

Glen Aulin High Sierra Camp

Young Lakes

Tioga Pass Entrance

Tuolumne Meadows

Tuolumne Meadows Visitor Center

Mt Dana

May Lake High Sierra Camp

Tuolumne Lodge

May Lake

Cathedral Peak

Elizabeth Lake

Mammoth Peak

Grant Lake

Tenaya Lake

Evelyn Lake

Olmsted Point

Sunrise High Sierra Camp

Vogelsang High Sierra Camp

Bernice Lake

June Lake

Merced Lake

Merced Lake High Sierra Camp

Mt Lyell

Merced River

Washburn Lake

Inyo National Forest

Mt Clark

Merced River

Edna Lake

Ottoway Lakes

Legend:
— Roads
- - - Trails
(P) Parking
Food
Gas
Ranger Station

Chain Lakes

Sierra National Forest

N

0   10 Miles

Established: October 1, 1890

Size: 748,542 acres, or 1,169 square miles; 94 percent of the park is designated wilderness.

Address: P.O. Box 577, Yosemite National Park, CA 95389

Campsites: 1,445 individual sites park-wide

Overnight accommodations: 1,386 units

Paved roads: 214 miles

Developed trails: 800 miles

Wildlife species (approximate):

Amphibians and reptiles: 40

Birds: More than 150 regularly occurring species

Fish: 6 native species

Mammals: Approximately 90

Flora species:

Flowering plants: 1,500

Trees: 35

Geographic center of the park: Mt. Hoffmann

Highest paved pass in the Sierra: Tioga Pass, 9,945 ft.

Major lakes: 318

With fish: 127

Without fish: 191

Rivers and streams: 880 miles

Park speed limit: 45 mph (unless otherwise posted)

Yosemite's Ten Highest Peaks

1. Mt. Lyell: 13,114 ft.
2. Mt. Dana: 13,053 ft.
3. Kuna Peak: 13,003 ft.
4. Rodgers Peak: 12,978 ft.
5. Mt. Maclure: 12,960 ft.
6. Mt. Gibbs: 12,764 ft.
7. Mt. Conness: 12,590 ft.
8. Mt. Florence: 12,561 ft.
9. Simmons Peak: 12,503 ft.
10. Excelsior Mountain: 12,446 ft.

Park Visitation

1855: 42

1899: 4,500

1922: 100,506

1940: 506,781

1954: 1,008,031

1995: 4,101,928

2000: 3,550,065

2010: 4,047,880

Entrance Fees

$20   Private Noncommercial Vehicles

$10   Bus Passengers, Bicyclists, and Persons on Foot or Horseback

$40   Annual Yosemite Pass

$80   America the Beautiful—National Parks and Federal Recreational Lands Pass (good at all national parks and federal recreation lands for one year from purchase date)

$10   America the Beautiful—National Parks and Federal Recreational Lands Pass, Senior Pass (a lifetime pass for US citizens 62 years and older), one-time issuance fee

Free: America the Beautiful—National Parks and Federal Recreational Lands Pass, Access Pass (for blind or permanently disabled US citizens or permanent residents)

Free: America the Beautiful—National Parks and Federal Recreational Lands Pass, Volunteer Pass (a one-year pass for volunteers who have acquired 500 service hours)

Important Yosemite Phone Numbers

Camping reservations 1-888-444-6777
(international callers)......... (518) 885-3639

Dental clinic .... (209) 372-4200

High Sierra Camp
reservations .... (801) 559-4909

Lost and found .... (209) 372-1390

Medical clinic..................... (209) 372-4637

Park information
(recorded) ....(209) 372-0200

Room reservations............. (801) 559-5000

Visitor Centers:

    Big Oak Flat.................. (209) 379-1899

    Tuolumne Meadows..... (209) 372-0263

    Wawona .... (209) 375-9531

Weather and road info ....(209) 372-0200

Wilderness reservations.... (209) 372-0740

Yosemite Conservancy
Warehouse Store .... (209) 379-2648

Emergencies 911

TDD Phones

These allow the hearing impaired with their own TDDs to call the park directly.

National Park Service
information .... (209) 372-4726

Room reservations............. (559) 252-2846

Camping reservations .... (877) 833-6777

Yosemite's climate is as mild as its cliffs are steep. The months of April through October feature warm daytime temperatures and cool nights. Even winter is relatively benign, with average maximum temperatures in Yosemite Valley (4,000 feet) in the high 40s and 50s. It does get cold in the shade of the granite walls, especially on the south side of the valley. Of course, weather is significantly affected by elevation, and with a topography ranging from 2,000 to 13,000 feet in height, Yosemite can experience amazing climatic variations on any given day! Precipitation averages 35 to 40 inches of moisture annually, with the bulk of that falling between December and March. Snowfall in Yosemite Valley averages 29 inches but rarely accumulates to a depth of over two feet. At 7,000-foot Badger Pass, there is adequate snowpack to support a downhill ski area, and cross-country skiing is popular throughout the higher regions of the park. As temperatures warm in the spring, increasing runoff swells rivers and creeks, producing a grand display of surging waterfalls. There is negligible precipitation during the summer months, and many of the park's waterfalls literally dry up. For Yosemite weather reports, call (209) 372-0200.

Yosemite Valley in Winter

High-country conditions are significantly cooler and much snowier during the winter months. For the latest weather conditions in Yosemite, visit http://www.nps.gov/yose/planyourvisit/conditions.htm.

Yosemite Valley Weather Data

	Jan	Feb	Mar	Apr	May	Jun	Jul	Aug	Sep	Oct	Nov	Dec
Rainfall in inches*	6.5	6.7	5.2	2.8	1.7	0.7	0.4	0.1	0.7	2.1	4.6	5.5
Max. temp. (°F)	48	52	58	64	71	81	89	89	82	71	56	47
Min. temp. (°F)	29	30	34	38	48	51	57	56	51	42	33	28

* 37 inches annually

	January	April	July	October
Hours of sunshine	3:57	7:38	9:34	6:45
Chances of a sunny day	39%	70%	97%	81%
Afternoon temperatures	48°	66°	90°	75°
Relative humidity	86%	69%	50%	64%
Chances of a dry day	74%	80%	97%	94%
Total precipitation	6.8"	3.3"	0.4"	1.5"
Snowfall	25.4"	4.5"	–	0.2"

Tent cabins at Curry Village in Yosemite Valley

Most overnight accommodations in Yosemite are operated by DNC Parks & Resorts at Yosemite, a contractor of the National Park Service and the park's chief concessioner. There is a single reservation system for all DNC lodging units. (If a Yosemite hotel or motel mentioned in this guidebook is not part of the DNC reservation system, that fact will be noted.) Reservations can be made by phone or online. (Note that reservations for High Sierra Camps or hotel suites must be made by telephone.) The DNC reservation number is (801) 559-5000. Because thousands of calls are made to this number each day, you may not get through when you phone. Be persistent: let the phone ring, and try, try again. Better yet, use the Internet. If you've got a credit card, visit www.yosemitepark.com to request your reservation online.

Seven Tips for Getting a Yosemite Reservation

1. Public reservations for Yosemite lodging open exactly 366 days in advance. Call the Yosemite Reservations office at (801) 559-5000 as early as 7 a.m. Pacific time exactly 366 days before your intended arrival. (801) 559-4884 immediately upon the opening of the Yosemite Reservations office (7 a.m. Pacific time) exactly 366 days before your intended arrival.

2. Choose to visit in Yosemite's off-season, particularly the months of November, January, February, and March. You're sure to be accommodated if your stay falls on weekdays.

3. If you want to stay over a weekend, plan your arrival for a Monday, Tuesday, Wednesday, or Thursday. You can reserve up to seven nights in a row in any given stay. Often, lodging facilities are fully reserved for weekends more than 366 days in advance by people arriving earlier in the week.

4. Be flexible and have several arrival dates in mind. If your first option is not available, one of the others may be.

5. If you're willing to stay in a tent cabin at Curry Village, request it. Tent cabins are in the least demand. They can usually be reserved up to two weeks before arrival—but are often sold out in the summer. When you arrive, you can always try to upgrade to a room with bath (but there are no guarantees here).

6. Weekends tend to be very busy. On weekdays most calls come in first thing in the morning or in the evening, with a slight uptick at lunch. In general, midday is the quietest and best time to call.

7. Cancellations happen all the time, with increasing frequency as the 7-day cancellation deadline approaches. Call in advance of your desired arrival date. You may get lucky.

Yosemite National Park offers visitors almost fifteen hundred campsites in its multiple campgrounds. If you're planning to camp, be sure to secure an authorized spot, because camping is allowed only in designated campsites. Even if you've got a "self-contained" recreational vehicle, you are not permitted to pull off to the side of the road for the night. Neither should you erect your tent or throw down a sleeping bag wherever you stop; the rangers will send you packing. The impact on the park resources of such haphazard camping is too great. Fortunately, there's a way to ensure that you'll have a Yosemite camping spot when you arrive. The majority of park campsites can be reserved through a campground reservation system called Recreation.gov. Throughout this guidebook, campgrounds with sites that can be reserved through this system are indicated.

How to Reserve Your Campsite

Campground reservations become available in one-month blocks up to five months in advance. Reservations can be made through Recreation.gov on the 15th of each month for this one-month "window." For example, on March 15, dates from July 15 through August 14 become available for reservation, and on April 15, dates from August 15 through September 14 are reservable (to ensure that you have the most up-to-date information about this, see http://www.nps.gov/yose/planyourvisit/camping.htm.) You can reserve campsites through Recreation.gov in two ways: over the Internet at www.recreation.gov, or by telephone at (877) 444-6777. The number for international callers is (518) 885-3639. Phone reservations can be made between 7 a.m. and 7 p.m. Pacific time. Nearly all successful reservations are made online—use the telephone only as a last resort.

The system allows callers to choose from a full month of starting dates for their camping trip. Be sure to pick a number of possible start dates for your trip and you should be able to secure a reservation. When making online camping reservations, you can reserve only two campsites at a time. Another website, www.yosemitesites.com, provides helpful information about how many tent sites are available in each campground and still reservable. For additional information about park campgrounds, refer to the following pages: Valley, page 96; South of Yosemite Valley, page 117; North of Yosemite Valley, page 138.

Camping in US Forest Service Areas adjacent to Yosemite

The US Forest Service operates a variety of campgrounds near Yosemite. Many of them are operated on a first-come, first-served basis; some sites can be reserved in advance. For additional information, call the appropriate USFS district office.

Inyo National Forest
Eastern Sierra, Highways 120 and 395
Mono Lake Ranger Station,
(760) 647-3044

Sierra National Forest
Western Sierra, Highways 140 and 41

Bass Lake Ranger District
Oakhurst Ranger Station,
(559) 877-2218

Mariposa Ranger Station,
(209) 966-3638

Stanislaus National Forest
Western Sierra, Highway 120

Groveland Ranger Station,
(209) 962-7825

Happy camper

Campground/General Location

There is a 30-day camping limit within Yosemite National Park in a calendar year; however, from May 1–September 15, the camping limit in Yosemite is 14 days, and only 7 of those days can be in Yosemite Valley or Wawona.

Campground/General Location	Sites/spaces	Daily fee	Max RV/Trailer size	Water	Toilets	Pets allowed	Dump station	Showers nearby	Laundry nearby	Groceries	Swimming	Fishing	Horseback riding	Season (approx)	Reservations
North Pines Yosemite Valley	81	$20	40 ft/35 ft.	Tap	Flush	•	•	•	•	•	•	•	•	April–Sept	Recreation.gov
Upper Pines Yosemite Valley	238	$20	35 ft/24 ft.	Tap	Flush	•	•	•	•	•	•	•	•	All year	Recreation.gov Mar 15–Nov; First come Dec–Mar 15
Lower Pines Yosemite Valley	60	$20	40 ft/35 ft	Tap	Flush	•	•	•	•	•	•	•	•	Mar–Oct	Recreation.gov
Camp 4 Yosemite Valley	35	$5/ person	No RVs/trailers	Tap	Flush			•	•	•	•	•		All year	First come
Backpackers Walk-In (see text) Yosemite Valley															
Wawona Wawona Road, Wawona	93	$20	35 ft/35 ft	Tap	Flush	near					•	•	•	All year	Recreation.gov Apr–Sept; First come Oct–Mar
Bridalveil Creek Glacier Point Road	110	$14	35 ft/24 ft	Tap	Flush	•						•	•	July–early Sept	First come
Hodgdon Meadow off Big Oak Flat Road near entrance	105	$20	40 ft/30 ft	Tap	Flush	•								All year	Recreation.gov Apr 15–Oct 15; First come Oct 15–Apr 15
Hetch Hetchy Backpacker (see text) Hetch Hetchy Rd															
Crane Flat Big Oak Flat Rd near Tioga Rd turnoff	166	$20	40 ft/30 ft	Tap	Flush	•								July–Sept	Recreation.gov
Tamarack Flat Tioga Road	52	$10	not recommended	Creek (boil)	Vault	•								July–Sept	First come
White Wolf Tioga Road	74	$14	27 ft/24 ft	Tap	Flush	•						•		July–early Sept	First come
Yosemite Creek Tioga Road	75	$10	not recommended	Creek (boil)	Vault	•						•		July–early Sept	First come
Porcupine Flat Tioga Road	52	$10	24 ft(ltd)/20 ft(ltd)	Creek (boil)	Vault									July–Oct 15	First come
Tuolumne Meadows Tioga Road	304	$20	35 ft/35 ft	Tap	Flush	•					•	•	•	July–late Sept	50% Recreation.gov, 50% first come

Because there are some eight hundred miles of trail in Yosemite ranging through some of the most stunning scenery in the world, backpacking is a popular activity in the park. It allows its practitioners a true wilderness experience, and it is really the only way to reach many areas of Yosemite.

A hiker in Yosemite

But successful, minimum-impact backpacking requires good physical health, knowledge of backpacking techniques, proper equipment, and a respect for the natural world. Uninformed backcountry users can cause great harm to the wilderness and not even know it. Here are some basic tips for backpackers, as well as wilderness regulations and sources for further information.

Get a Wilderness Permit

Free wilderness permits are required year-round for all overnight stays in Yosemite's backcountry. To avoid overcrowding and reduce impacts to wilderness areas, Yosemite limits the number of people who may begin overnight hikes from each trailhead each day. At least 40 percent of each trailhead quota is available on a first-come, first-served basis the day of, or one day prior to, the beginning of your trip.

These permits can be obtained at any of the following locations in the park: the Wilderness Center in Yosemite Valley (just east of the Visitor Center); Tuolumne Meadows Wilderness Center (just off the Tioga Road on the road to Tuolumne Lodge); Wawona Visitor Center (see page 107); Big Oak Flat Information Station (see page 125); and Hetch Hetchy Entrance Station, for those using Hetch Hetchy trails (see page 125).

Wilderness permit reservations can now be made year-round, from up to twenty-four weeks to two days in advance.

Besides visiting the Wilderness Center, those desiring a reservation can mail in a reservation request, visit the Wilderness Reservation website (http://www.nps.gov/yose/planyourvisit/wildpermits.htm/), or call the center at (209) 372-0740. You can also print out a reservation form from the above website and fax it to (209) 372-0739. A non-refundable fee of $5 plus $5 per person is charged for reservations. Fees can be paid by check (payable to "Yosemite Conservancy") or with a major credit card (include the expiration date).

The following information is needed to process a wilderness permit or reservation: name, address, daytime phone; number of people in group; method of travel (e.g., ski, snowshoe, foot, horse); starting and ending dates of hike; the entry and exit trailhead you use; your primary destination; number of pack stock (if applicable); and alternative dates or trailheads if your first choice isn't available. Mail requests should be sent to Wilderness Center, P.O. Box 545, Yosemite, CA 95389.

Permits can be picked up no sooner than 24 hours prior to trailhead departure. Reservations are especially recommended for hikes leaving from Tuolumne Meadows or with destinations of Little Yosemite Valley, Half Dome, or Merced Lake, and for any hikers planning a Saturday-night stay.

Wilderness Regulations

Group Size
Maximum group size in the Yosemite Wilderness is 15 people on trails, and 8 people for any off-trail travel.

Campsite Location
Please use existing campsites at least one hundred feet from lakeshores and streams to minimize pollution and impact on vegetation. Camp at least four trail-miles from Tuolumne Meadows, Yosemite Valley, Glacier Point, White Wolf, Hetch Hetchy, and Wawona, and at least one mile from any road.

Human Waste
Bury human waste six inches deep in a small hole at least 100 feet from any lake, stream, or camp area. Toilet paper should be packed out.

Garbage
Pack out all garbage (no exceptions). Do not bury garbage, scatter organic waste, or leave foil in campfire sites.

Fires

Use gas stoves rather than wood fires. Wood fires are not permitted above 9,600 feet due to firewood scarcity. Use only existing fire rings and dead and down wood in areas below 9,600 feet.

Pets

Dogs and other pets are not allowed in the Yosemite Wilderness.

Soap

Putting soap, including biodegradable soap, or any form of pollutant into lakes or streams is prohibited. Discard wash and rinse water at least 100 feet from water sources.

Route-Planning Information

Space considerations preclude listing the thousands of trips that can be made into the Yosemite Wilderness. But never fear, there are many resources available to help with your route-planning task. You can obtain maps or trail guides from the Yosemite Conservancy, at the Wilderness Center, at one of the Visitor Center bookstores, through the Yosemite Bookstore online at www.yosemiteconservancystore.com, through the mail by writing P.O. Box 230, El Portal, CA 95318, or by calling (209) 379-2648.

Hiking near May Lake

Wilderness Tips

Visit the Wilderness Center

At the Wilderness Center, just east of the Visitor Center on the pedestrian mall in Yosemite Valley, detailed information is available about the park's wilderness. There are educational displays and a trip-planning section, and guidebooks, maps, and backpacking supplies are offered for sale. For additional information, visit the NPS wilderness information website at http://www.nps.gov/yose/planyourvisit/backpacking.htm.

Key Phone Numbers

Wilderness permit reservations: (209) 372-0740

Current wilderness conditions: (209) 372-0308

Tuolumne Meadows Wilderness Center: (209) 372-0309

Wilderness permit late arrivals/cancellations: (209) 372-0308

For more information about making reservations or obtaining a permit: (209) 372-0740.

For information about wilderness conditions, check http://www.nps.gov/yose/planyourvisit/wildcond.htm

Treat the Water

Unfortunately, microscopic organisms known as *Giardia lamblia* (see page 78) are present in wilderness lakes, rivers, and streams. They can cause illness (sometimes quite severe), so you should not drink from these sources without first treating the water. Your options are to boil it for three minutes, to use a chemical disinfectant like iodine or chlorine (less effective than boiling), or to use the Giardia-rated water filters available from outdoor equipment stores and at the Wilderness Center.

Get Acclimatized

Many wilderness trips begin at elevations much higher than you may be accustomed to, and then go even higher. It's a good idea to arrive a day early to let your body adapt to the thinner air. Don't over-exert, make sure you eat enough, and drink plenty of fluids to avoid altitude sickness.

Bear-Proof Your Campsite

Yosemite's black bears are clever and very persistent. If you fail to set up your camp and store your food properly, your whole trip may be ruined. Always follow these six steps:

1. Use the food storage boxes at your trailhead for storing any food that you will not be taking on your backpack trip. Never leave food or food-related supplies in vehicles left overnight at trailheads. Even toothpaste or deodorant can smell like food to a bear. Along with their keen sense of smell, bears are immensely strong. They will peel down your rear door, rip out the back seat, and crawl into the trunk to get food. They can smell food even if it's hidden from sight, and they know what coolers look like.

2. Store your food in a bear-resistant food storage container. Weighing just 2.9 pounds and holding from 5 to 7 days' worth of food for one person, the canisters are required by the National Park Service. Bears aside, canisters are proof against birds, marmots, and the many other creatures that will happily eat your food. (Visit any Information Center, Wilderness Center, or Visitor Center for more information.)

3. Do not hang your food—it is illegal and ineffective. Even if you somehow manage to hang it from a limb inaccessible to a small, agile bear,

squirrels, raccoons, and birds will definitely be able to get it.

4. If a bear approaches your camp, act immediately to scare it away. Yell and make as much noise as possible, and scare the bear. It's more effective if more than one person chases the bear. Throw small rocks no larger than acorns at the bear, but make sure that you do not hurt it—the bear is not trying to harm you. A big rock will hurt a bear just as it would hurt a human.

Black bear cub

5. Always maintain a distance. Do not advance on a bear that appears to feel threatened or cornered by you. Do not attempt to retrieve food or gear until the bear abandons it.

6. Food taken by bears is your responsibility. Please clean up and report all bear damage to a ranger. Improper food storage can cause not only personal injury and property loss, but death of conditioned bears. Please do your part to keep Yosemite's bears wild.

Going Green

Climate change is an issue everywhere. Some of its impacts, however, are more striking and relevant in Yosemite than in other parts of the country. These include impacts to the snow line and wildlife. Both are retreating farther up the mountains as time goes by.

The view from Glacier Point

Yosemite's long history as a tourist destination means that it enjoys a richer photographic record than many mountain areas. Old pictures reveal broad glaciers and tourists tobogganing and skiing through a snow-blanketed Yosemite Valley. It still snows in Yosemite Valley sometimes, but a typical winter storm now turns from rain to snow at about 5,500 feet, leaving a dusting in the valley that quickly melts away. Of course this development disappoints tourists who arrive in January expecting to see the winter, but there are more serious concerns. The snows of the Sierra Nevada melt in the spring, providing most of the water for agriculture in California. Thus the diminution of the snowpack has serious repercussions for the farmers of the Central Valley, and for everyone who eats their food. A quarter of the nation's food crops come from the Central Valley.

The retreating snowpack goes hand in hand with retreating wildlife. In the 1910s and 1920s, biologist Joseph Grinnell made a thorough survey of Yosemite's ecosystems, painstakingly recording the presence and abundance of animals across a gigantic transect from the Central Valley across the park and east to Mono Lake. Now, in a large-scale, multiyear project, UC Berkeley is redoing Grinnell's survey. They have found that animals, especially small ones such as alpine chipmunks and pikas, are moving upslope, away from the heat. With less living space and less food available at higher elevations, the impact of climate change on these populations may be dire.

During your time in Yosemite, it may not be within your power to increase the snowpack or provide a home for a pika. There are things you can do, though, to limit your impact. The most obvious is to take free shuttle buses to your destinations. With a little planning, you can get to most of the places in the park by bus, and for a lot less than you would have spent on gas. If you're staying in Yosemite Valley, you can easily reach most of the valley floor by bicycle, either your own or a rental bike from Curry Village. If you're camping, consider whether you really want to build that gigantic bonfire—much of the carbon in the atmosphere comes from burning wood. Summer days often find Yosemite Valley filled with smoky haze from hundreds of campfires.

When you go out to eat, pay attention to the options on the menu. Many of the park's restaurants, such as those at the Ahwahnee, the Yosemite Lodge, and the Wawona Hotel, feature dining options that were organically grown, which means minimal oil-based fertilizer. And these foods come from areas near the park, requiring a lot less energy to be transported from the farm to your plate than do similar meals grown far away. They are also fresher and often taste better.

A Ranger Is a Ranger Is a...

Yosemite National Park is administered by the US National Park Service (NPS), an agency of the Department of the Interior established in 1916. As a bureaucracy based loosely on a military model, the NPS is characterized by a complex ordering of job ranks and by its distinctive field uniforms. The green pants, gray shirt, and universally recognized "Smokey Bear" hat have become the trademark of the park ranger. The key descriptor here is "park," as park rangers differ from forest rangers. Forest rangers work for the US Forest Service, a branch of the US Department of Agriculture, in national forests throughout the country. While the job duties of park and forest rangers are often similar in their respective situations, park rangers work in parks and monuments, and forest rangers work in _____ (you fill in the blank!).

Now that you're able to recognize that the person in the flat-brimmed hat before you is a park ranger working in a national park, things start to get a bit more complicated. The National Park Service is divided into any number of departments that range in purpose from visitor protection to interpretation to maintenance to resource management to administration. Confusing things further, employees of the different divisions all wear roughly the same uniform. The traditional park ranger is employed by the Division of Visitor Protection, with duties that include law enforcement, traffic regulation, search and rescue, emergency medical treatment, and many others. In order to work as a traditional park ranger, one must take special training and earn a law enforcement commission.

Park interpreters (interpretive rangers, formerly called naturalists) are responsible for the educational walks, talks, and other such programs at Yosemite. They, too, are rangers, but they generally have not been commissioned and do not perform law enforcement functions. Their uniforms are identical to those of protection rangers, but they don't carry guns and handcuffs.

Identical, too, are the outfits of the various park administrators, such as the superintendent (the park's chief administrative officer), deputy superintendent, chief ranger, and other division chiefs. An easy way to distinguish these management types is by their skin pallor. They attend so many government meetings they almost never see the sun.

Things get a little more confusing with certain maintenance, fire, and resource management workers. They've got the green pants, ditto the gray shirt, but instead of the funny hat, they wear dark green baseball caps with the NPS arrowhead insignia. These employees are not technically rangers, but their roles at Yosemite are equally significant.

Most people don't realize that the National Park Service has exclusive jurisdiction over Yosemite National Park. That means that state, county, and local agencies do not operate here, and they provide almost no services here: in Yosemite there are no highway patrol officers, no sheriff's officers, no state or municipal firefighters, no state courts, and no incorporated local government. These services fall to the National Park Service, which very ably manages the park.

Please remember while you're in the park, if you need help of any kind (from emergency assistance to information), that all uniformed NPS personnel are there to be of service.

A Yosemite ranger on horseback

Many people have the impression that when the first day of winter arrives in Yosemite, the whole place closes up tight until spring. They are mistaken, however; the park and its residents do not hibernate, except for the bears. Yosemite only "closes" when deep snowfall makes it impossible to plow access roads (which is almost never).

There are notable park changes in winter, but most of them add to the unique qualities of this special season. Much of Yosemite wears a covering of snow, and once-thundering waterfalls quiet themselves in frozen dormancy. Tioga Road and Glacier Point Road close, and visitor activities center on such winter sports as skiing and skating.

Weekdays in winter are perfect for experiencing Yosemite in an uncrowded, serene environment. Yosemite Valley daytime temperatures can be surprisingly mild, and winter walks are some of the best. The biggest reward of all, however, is the sheer beauty and grandeur of a transfigured Yosemite and the surrounding high country.

The major routes to the park remain open throughout the year. The roadway least affected by the weather is Highway 140, which leads from Merced via Mariposa and through the Arch Rock Entrance to the park. Highways 120 (from the west) and 41 are also excellent routes, but they are more often subject to closure from heavy snowfall, and use of tire chains is frequently required on them. The roads in Yosemite Valley are plowed throughout the winter.

Winter driving in Yosemite requires special precautions. Because roads are regularly covered with ice and snow, driving speeds should be reduced. You may be required to carry tire chains in your vehicle—whether or not you have four-wheel drive—depending on conditions. Watch out for snowplows, and never stop in the roadway (find a pullout where traffic can safely pass).

Skiing and Snowboarding

Both cross-country types and downhillers will discover ski and snowboard opportunities in Yosemite. California's oldest operating ski area, Badger Pass, is located at 7,300 feet, about forty-five minutes from Yosemite Valley on Glacier Point Road. It's primarily a "family" oriented operation with nine runs and four ski lifts. Badger

is an ideal place to learn to ski, and a ski school is available. Free shuttle buses to Badger Pass are provided during the winter from lodging facilities in Yosemite Valley (and from other points on busy weekends). Call (209) 372-4FUN (4386) for information about Badger Pass and the shuttle.

Miles and miles of both groomed and ungroomed trails for cross-country skiers also originate at Badger Pass. Tracks are laid out on Glacier Point Road, sometimes all the way to Glacier Point, and skating lanes are also provided. Well-signed trails lead into the wilderness and out to the south rim of Yosemite Valley. The cross-country ski school at Badger offers classes, individualized instruction, and guided tours. Phone (209) 372-8444 or visit http://www.badgerpass.com/ for details.

A variety of services are available at the Badger Pass Ski Lodge: snowboard and ski rentals (both downhill and cross-country), ski repair, child care, and food and beverage service. There's also a locker room and restrooms. The National Park Service staffs a ranger station, primarily as a first-aid facility, in the A-frame building at Badger. The phone number is (209) 372-0409.

Another popular cross-country ski area is Crane Flat, located at the intersection of Big Oak Flat and Tioga Roads, seventeen miles from Yosemite Valley. There are no services provided here, but the meadows and forests are full of trails for skiers and snowshoers.

Snowshoeing

You can snowshoe on your own wherever there's adequate snow (at Badger Pass, Crane Flat, or the Mariposa Big Trees, for example), or enjoy a ranger-led snowshoe walk on which the snowshoes are provided. Walks are presented several days a week,

Bridalveil Fall in winter

starting in front of the A-frame at Badger Pass, and reservations are required. Check *Yosemite Guide* or call (209) 372-0409.

Ice Skating

A large outdoor ice rink is operated daily in Yosemite Valley at Curry Village (weather permitting) from November through March. It features a smooth, refrigerated skating surface, rental skates, a warming hut with lockers, a fire pit, and a snack stand. For hours and rates call (209) 372-8341.

Snow Play

Provisions have been made for individuals and families with a passion for sledding, tobogganing, inner-tubing, and snow play generally. The designated area for these activities in Yosemite is at the Crane Flat Campground on Big Oak Flat Road near its intersection with Tioga Road. Another good snow-play area is found just south of the park on Highway 41 at Goat Meadow, in the Sierra National Forest. There is also sledding on the medial moraine, near the Yosemite Valley stables. Supervise children well, and be careful of sliding into roadways. Many injuries related to snow play occur every year.

Camping

There are four campgrounds in Yosemite that are open for use during winter. In Yosemite Valley, both Upper Pines Campground and Camp 4 (see page 96) have been winterized. The Wawona Campground (see page 117) is the winter camping area south of the valley, and in the north end of the park, it's Hodgdon Meadow Campground (see page 138). All these campgrounds are first-come, first-served.

Backcountry Ski Huts

For the intrepid wilderness skier, three different huts are operated in Yosemite's backcountry. Nine miles from Badger Pass to the south of Glacier Point Road is the Ostrander Lake Ski Hut. Set on the banks of a deeply frozen lake and below scenic Horse Ridge, the hut can accommodate up to twenty-five skiers overnight. There are beds with mattresses, cooking facilities, toilets, a wood stove, and water. Run by the Yosemite Conservancy, the Ostrander Ski Hut is so popular that reservations are required. Call (209) 372-0740 for details, or write Ostrander Reservations, P.O. Box 545, Yosemite NP, CA 95389. Also check www.yosemiteconservancy.org.

Winter in Wawona

The second hut is located at Glacier Point and is reached by skiing the ten miles out from Badger Pass to the end of Glacier Point Road. It is operated by DNC, which also requires reservations. Beds and meals are provided, and a guide will accompany you and do the cooking. To learn more about the Glacier Point Hut call (209) 372-8444 or visit http://www.yosemitepark.com/badgerpass_crosscountryskiing_glacierpointhut.aspx.

The Tuolomne Meadows Ski Hut is open until the Tioga Road opens in the spring. It sleeps ten and is available at no charge, first-come, first-served. The hut is the stone building right at the entrance to the Tuolomne Meadows Campground, approximately eight miles west of Tioga Pass. The NPS operates but does not staff this ski hut. Be prepared to camp out if the hut is full.

The Bracebridge Dinner

Perhaps Yosemite's most long-standing winter tradition is the Bracebridge Dinner. A multi-course Christmas feast is presented at the Ahwahnee Hotel in the context of a colorful pageant based loosely on Washington Irving's account in *The Sketch Book of Geoffrey Crayon, Gent.* of a typical Yorkshire Christmas dinner in the manor of Squire Bracebridge. The music, costumes, food, and drama combine for an unforgettable experience. Tickets for the event (held multiple times) are in great demand, and reservations for the dinner are much sought after. Reservations are accepted beginning the first Tuesday of February every year. For more information or to reserve tickets to Bracebridge, call (801) 559-5000. For the 2011 dinners, tickets were $425 per person (including taxes and gratuity).

A public shower?

In Yosemite Valley, there are showers at Curry Village (open all year) and at Housekeeping Camp (closed in winter). There are no public showers in Wawona. There is a fee for all showers.

A laundromat?

The only park laundromat (open all year) is at Housekeeping Camp in Yosemite Valley.

A post office?

In Yosemite Valley, the main post office is in Yosemite Village (near the Visitor Center). There is a year-round post office in the Wawona Store, and a summer-only post office in Tuolumne Meadows at the grocery store.

An ATM?

In Yosemite Valley, there are ATMs in Yosemite Village, inside the Village Store and to the south of the store at the Yosemite Art Center; at Yosemite Lodge, inside the main registration area; and at Curry Village, inside the gift/grocery store. In Wawona, the ATM is inside the Wawona Store, and at Tuolumne Meadows, it's inside the grocery store.

A babysitter?

Limited babysitting is available for registered guests at Yosemite Lodge and the Ahwahnee. Call the front desk or see the concierge for additional information.

A dog kennel?

The only park kennel is in Yosemite Valley, at the DNC stables. Dogs must be gentle, weigh over twenty pounds (smaller may be okay if you provide a portable kennel), and have proof of shots and a license. Call (209) 372-8348 for more information.

A copy machine or a fax machine?

In Yosemite Valley, contact the front desk at Yosemite Lodge, Curry Village, or the Ahwahnee. A fee is charged for these services.

A good time?

If you're not enjoying yourself in Yosemite, with all it has to offer, you need to see your therapist.

A cup of coffee?

In Yosemite Valley, visit the Food Court at Yosemite Lodge, Degnan's Deli in the village, and the Coffee Corner at Curry Village.

A cold beer?

There are three real bars in Yosemite, both in Yosemite Valley. The Ahwahnee Bar is probably the classiest spot in the park, with a fine selection of wine, liquor, and mixed drinks in an elegant setting. The Mountain Room, at the Yosemite Lodge, is slightly more casual but does have a pleasant atmosphere and a wide selection of drinks. Curry Village also has a bar.

There is no actual bar at the Wawona Hotel, but a full drink selection is available there. You can enjoy a cocktail in their comfortable lounge or with dinner.

For a very casual atmosphere, almost a sports-bar feel, Degnan's Pizza Loft, above Degnan's Deli, has some wines and usually a pretty good selection of beers, both in the bottle and on tap. In the winter months this switches over to an employees-only hangout. There is also a bar attached to the Yosemite View Lodge restaurant, just outside the park. The View Lodge store also has an impressive beer section, but it is expensive.

Most of the sit-down restaurants in Yosemite serve drinks and have a few beers on tap. If all you're looking for, though, is a fine beer at the end of the day and you don't want to go to the effort and expense of a bar or restaurant, your best bet is to buy a few bottles or a six-pack from the Village Store or the Tuolumne Store and take it back to your campsite or wherever you're staying.

Outdoor dining at the Ahwahnee Hotel

A picnic in Yosemite Valley

Groceries and Supplies

Most people don't come to Yosemite to go shopping. But when your needs turn from natural beauty to a hearty meal or cold drink, you need not fear. The park is well supplied with grocery stores as well as other modern conveniences. Of course the stores sell camping food and souvenirs, but if you look you can find anything that you might want (within reason) in the park. Be aware that you'll pay a little more than you would at home. Head to the following places to satisfy your needs.

The Yosemite Village Store and the Tuolumne Store (open only in summer) are much like traditional grocery stores. The Village Store is by far the best grocery option in the park. Yosemite locals do a fair amount of their grocery shopping here. It features a surprisingly strong wine rack and beer selection, and a good amount of organic food. The Tuolumne Store is smaller, but it has enough for you to base your summer trip out of Tuolumne Meadows on and not have to go to the valley to buy anything.

The Curry Village Store, Yosemite Lodge Store, and Wawona Store carry limited supplies but are all good options.

There are several locations where you can find snack food: the Crane Flat Gas Station, Glacier Point Store, White Wolf Store, Wawona Golf Course Pro Shop, Mariposa Grove Gift Shop, Yosemite View Lodge Store. All are open only in the summer season except the Crane Flat Gas Station and Yosemite View Lodge.

Golden-mantled ground squirrel

What Can I Do with My Children?

Though just being in Yosemite should be enough to keep young people occupied and engaged, there are lots of activities and programs that will enhance their visit to the park. During your stay, be sure to check the *Yosemite Guide* newspaper for scheduled events that are specially designed for kids.

Take a Hike

With just about every park locale offering flat to moderate walking, a family hike is a great way to burn youthful energy and to reach undeveloped, uncrowded spots with remarkable views and natural beauty. Take a picnic and make a day of it! See pages 92, 93, 94, 112, 114, 116, 126, 130, and 136 for hiking ideas.

Enjoy a Bike Ride

The best park bicycle riding is in Yosemite Valley, which features miles of bike trails. Bring your own, or rent bicycles at Yosemite Lodge or Curry Village. See page 89 for details. Don't forget your helmets—you can rent them along with your bikes.

Visit Happy Isles

The Nature Center at Happy Isles in Yosemite Valley, open in summer only, is devoted to kids and the Junior Ranger program, with wildlife exhibits, nightlife display, and other presentations. There are books for sale, and Explorer Packs on a variety of topics can be checked out. They include activities designed to help children learn more about the natural world they live in. See page 90.

Help Them Become Junior Rangers

There are two self-guided "junior ranger" programs for kids in Yosemite. Children 3 through 6 can become "Little Cubs" and earn a button by completing the activities set out in *The Little Cub Handbook,* available at visitor centers throughout the park. The *Junior Ranger Handbook* is for those aged 7 to 13, and completion of the program allows them to become Junior Rangers and receive a certificate and patch. Any questions? Check with a ranger for more information.

Explore the Indian Village and Yosemite Museum

Within the Yosemite Museum in Yosemite Valley, a room has been dedicated to the culture of the local Native American people. Besides a number of educational displays, there is often someone demonstrating basket making or some other cultural aspect of the Miwok and Paiute people. Behind the museum is a garden area that includes exhibits about the local Native Americans.

Take in a Campfire Program

What better way to finish off a day than attending a traditional campfire program? During the summer, there are usually programs offered by rangers in campgrounds throughout the park. Check the *Yosemite Guide* newspaper for schedules.

You can also have a campfire at your own campsite. Make sure that you are aware of campfire regulations. You can buy wood, hot dogs, and s'mores material at the Yosemite Village Store.

Visit the Skating Rink

From November through March when weather allows, an outdoor ice rink operates at Curry Village beneath the shadow of Glacier Point. You can rent ice skates, and there's a warming hut as well as lockers, a fire pit, and a snack bar. The phone number is (209) 372-8319 or visit http://www.yosemitepark.com/Activities_WinterActivities_IceSkatingRink.aspx.

Engage in Snow Play

During winter, grab your sleds, toboggans, and inner tubes and head to the snow-play areas at the Crane Flat Campground or just outside the South Entrance at Goat Meadow on Highway 41. Relatively gentle and clear slopes afford hours of slipping and sliding.

Go Skiing or Snowboarding

The ski area at Badger Pass is perfect for families, with nine runs, multiple lifts, and lessons offered by a first-rate ski school. Rental equipment is available for snowboarding and downhill and cross-country skiing. See page 22.

Snowshoe with a Ranger

Snowshoe walks are offered at Badger Pass by National Park Service rangers for adults and children 10 years and older. Rental snowshoes are available. Check the *Yosemite Guide* newspaper for schedules.

If You Have Only One Day in Yosemite

If by some horrible twist of your itinerary you find yourself with but a single day in Yosemite National Park, you will be sorely cheated. The park is so large and so studded with fascinating features that usually three or four days are required to really "do the place justice." But take heart, for there are some remarkable highlights that can be enjoyed in a day, many of them centered in Yosemite Valley.

While Yosemite Valley's seven square miles comprise but a tiny fraction of the park's total area, they are jam-packed with spectacular scenic beauty. First of all, get out of your car (follow signs to day-use parking at Camp 6 near Yosemite Village) and board a free Yosemite Valley shuttle bus. Buses stop at practically every point of interest in the eastern end of Yosemite Valley, and they are the only means (besides bicycle or on foot) to enter the areas there that are closed to automobile traffic. Listed below are several activities that can be enjoyed in a day from stops along the shuttle bus route. See page 87 for more information on free shuttle buses. You might also consider taking a Yosemite Valley Floor Tour: operated by the park's concessioner (but with a ranger doing the talking) and leaving from Yosemite Lodge, the flatbed trailer tour covers many popular sites.

Valley Visitor Center

Here is a logical starting point for your visit. See page 86. Park information, an orientation film, exhibits, and books are all available here. If time allows, take in the Yosemite Museum Gallery and the Indian Cultural Exhibit, and walk through the Indian Village behind the center. (15 minutes to 2 hours)

Lower Yosemite Fall

Walk from the bus stop to the base of Lower Yosemite Fall—about a quarter of a mile. See page 92. Be prepared to get wet in spring when runoff is at its peak; in any season you'll be impressed by the imposing height of one of the world's most famous falls. (30 minutes to 1 hour)

Happy Isles

This is the trailhead for hikes to Vernal and Nevada falls, Half Dome, and other high-country destinations (except in winter). Walk to the Vernal Fall bridge (seven-tenths of a mile) for a breathtaking view of this beautiful cataract, or continue on to the top of the fall (if you've got the energy). This route is known as the Mist Trail for reasons that will be obvious. During the summer, the Nature Center at Happy Isles offers exhibits and books. This location also serves as the Junior Ranger Center. There are snacks at the kiosk behind the Happy Isles Shuttle Stop (1 to 3 hours)

Mirror Lake

From the shuttle bus stop, Mirror Lake is a half-mile walk up a slight grade. See page 92. While the lake only offers the mirrorlike surface for which it was named in spring and early summer (it's filling up with silt), one of the best views of Half Dome is to be had from its banks. The hike around the lake is easy and rewarding. (1 to 2 hours)

Yosemite Falls

Bridalveil Fall

Take the free shuttle bus or follow road signs to Wawona Road (toward Wawona and Fresno). Immediately after turning onto Wawona Road, turn left into the Bridalveil Fall parking lot. The short trail leads to the base of the fall, where a sheet of water floats downward 620 feet to the valley floor. (15 to 45 minutes)

Tunnel View

Turn left back onto Wawona Road and drive approximately three miles to the Tunnel View turnout, which is just below the entrance to the Wawona Tunnel. Before you will be the classic panoramic view of Yosemite Valley that greeted the first visitors here. (10 to 30 minutes)

The view from Glacier Point

Glacier Point

A 32-mile drive from Yosemite Valley, Glacier Point is unquestionably a "must see" for visitors with limited time. Within 200 yards of the parking lot is the top of the sheer southern wall of Yosemite Valley. Not only does the valley lie 3,200 feet below you, but also the entire park is revealed, with astounding vistas in every direction. Most of Yosemite's major peaks are identified, and exhibits explain the geologic processes that created this amazing landscape. There is probably no better view reachable by automobile of Yosemite Valley and the surrounding high country. The road to Glacier Point is closed in winter. See page 115 for more information. (1 hour for the drive from Yosemite Valley, and 30 minutes to 1 hour at Glacier Point)

Mariposa Grove of Big Trees

If you have already seen Yosemite Valley and Glacier Point and you've still got time (hard to believe!), the Mariposa Grove of Big Trees is located near the park's south entrance from Highway 41. See page 113. This magnificent stand of sequoias is Yosemite's largest and includes trees thousands of years old. A tram system transports visitors into the grove for a fee (from May to October), or you may enter on foot. (The hike into the upper grove area is fairly rigorous.) A small museum is open during the summer (the tram stops there), and famous trees, like the Grizzly Giant and the fallen Tunnel Tree, should not be missed. (2 to 3 hours)

Tuolumne Meadows and Tioga Road

Open in summer and early fall only, Tioga Road bisects the park and leads through Tuolumne Meadows, a beautiful subalpine meadow surrounded by soaring granite crags and polished domes (see page 133). If your trip out of the park takes you to the east, you will be able to enjoy the scenery lining Tioga Road and the exhibits describing it (see page 128). Be sure to stop at Olmsted Point for its remarkable view of Tenaya Canyon and the back side of Half Dome, and of Tenaya Lake, the deep-blue, icy-cold waters of which form Yosemite's largest natural lake. (2 to 2 ½ hours for the trip from Yosemite Valley to Tioga Pass)

Just Passing Through?

If it happens that you are simply driving through Yosemite (a regrettable situation), be sure to stop by a Visitor or Information Center, located at or near every park entrance, for recommendations from park staff on what to see.

Yosemite Climbing

Because of its granite landscape, Yosemite is a mecca for rock climbers from all over the United States and the world. Climbs range from short routes of 50 feet or less (a pitch) to multi-day ascents of Yosemite's biggest walls (like El Capitan), which are made up of many pitches. Yosemite Valley has been the location of so many climbing developments and innovations that it has become the yardstick against which all other climbing areas are measured. In every season of the year, climbers can be seen clinging to rock faces or hanging by their hands and feet from upward-leading cracks.

Passionate rock climbers populate a world foreign to most "normal" people and have developed a subculture with customs, clothing, language, and tools of its own. In Yosemite, that world revolves around Camp 4. Across Northside Drive from Yosemite Lodge, Camp 4 is the climbers' permanent temporary home. Its role in the evolution of rock climbing has been recognized by the United States government, and Camp 4 is on the National Register of Historic Places. Many of the hardcore climbers move to Tuolumne Meadows during the summer.

Not that long ago, climbers utilized many artificial techniques to accomplish their climbs. These included drilling holes in the rock and inserting permanent metal bolts, chiseling holds in the rocks, and hammering in steel pitons that damaged the rock and could not always be removed. Such techniques made certain routes climbable that might not otherwise be.

Today, a less destructive and harmful climbing ethic has developed. Bolts are placed much less often, chiseling is frowned upon, and high-tech devices like "chocks," "friends," and "cams" that are inserted into cracks and easily removed provide protection for climbers. It's known as "clean climbing," and it's a matter of high priority for climbers who wish to protect and preserve a natural climbing environment.

This cleaner, less invasive style is also called "trad" (for "traditional") climbing. Yosemite's vertical crack systems have allowed climbers to pioneer the style without taking unacceptable risks. The climbing community has been and continues to be split over the issue of how much bolting, if any, is acceptable.

Overall, trad climbing is more of an American style—European geology makes it harder to place removable safety gear. Hand in hand (or hand in granite) with this cleaner style came the rise of free climbing. Climbing free means propelling yourself up a route without pulling on the rope, or using artificial aid for anything other than arresting a fall. Most Yosemite climbing is done free, but using artificial means remains the standard on long, demanding routes up the valley's big walls.

Climbers on Lost Arrow Spire with Yosemite Falls behind them

For example, the Nose on El Capitan, perhaps the most iconic route in American climbing, is done many times a year using aid, but it has only been "freed" by a few of the best climbers in the world. The first free ascent of the Nose, in 1993 by the magnificent Lynn Hill, is considered one of the greatest achievements in climbing history.

For climbers not sufficiently challenged by free climbing, there is free soloing, in which climbers ascend a route in much the same way that children ascend a jungle gym—with no protective gear of any kind. Many of Yosemite's landmarks have been free soloed in less than a day. This book does not recommend free soloing. While most roped climbing is very safe if done properly, one small mistake can kill you if you climb unroped.

One interesting aspect of the climbing subculture is its system of naming and rating climbing routes. The first climber to successfully undertake a new path up a section of rock (a "first ascent") is entitled to name that route. That climber,

camp out on ledges thousands of feet above the ground.

Climbing Yosemite, off of Daff

While Yosemite is filled with climbable granite, El Capitan is the one feature that dominates all others, to climbers and lay-people alike. For decades, no one thought it would ever be climbed. But in 1958, after forty-seven unbelievably strenuous days on the wall, Warren Harding clambered up the Nose, ensuring that our twenty-ninth president can only ever be the second-greatest man named Warren Harding. Nowadays a typical team spends four days climbing the route. The current speed record, set in November 2010, is 2 hours, 36 minutes, and 27 seconds. If you visit Yosemite in spring or fall, you may be able to pick out climbers, tiny against the rock, gliding (or lurching) their way up El Capitan. Bring binoculars to El Capitan Meadow and look for the flash of sunlight on metal gear. If you go by at night, check for the headlamps as teams

and those who come after, attempt to rate the difficulty of climbing that route. The Yosemite Decimal System is used for this purpose and is an elaborate scale with ratings from 5.0 to 5.13 with grades from "a" to "d" at each level signifying different degrees of difficulty.

The technology of climbing has advanced considerably over the past several decades. Special ropes made from synthetic fibers are used, and they stretch to absorb the weight of a falling climber. Their strength under pressure has also increased. Shoes covered with sticky rubber that adheres to practically any surface are now commonly used. And devices such as cams made from high-strength alloys have expanded climbing opportunities as well.

But good equipment or not, climbers must still have the skill and strength to climb

Climbing a sheer rock face

the rocks. The mastery that has been achieved by many "rock jocks" is astounding, and routes that many once considered unclimbable are now accomplished almost daily. New routes are being explored and climbed, and other climbing firsts, like paraplegic Mark Wellman's 1989 ascent of El Capitan, continue to occur.

Rock climbing is not recommended for the casual park visitor. If you would like to learn more about the sport, consider taking a lesson from the Yosemite Mountaineering School either in Yosemite Valley, at (209) 372-8344, or in Tuolumne Meadows: summer only, call (209) 372-8435. Without proper equipment and without proper technique, you could severely injure yourself or die.

Very Curious Names for Yosemite Climbing Routes

Agricultural Maneuvers in the Dark (5.8)

Chairman Ted Scraps the Time Machine (5.10a)

Colony of Slippermen (5.11d)

Dope Smoking Moron (5.11)

Gerbil Launcher (5.10d)

God Told Me to Skin You Alive (5.11a)

Public Enema Number One (5.11c)

Stand and Quiver (5.11a)

Tooth or Consequences (5.11b)

Vegetal Extraction (5.10)

Aunt Fanny's Pantry (5.4)

Try Again Ledge (5.8)

Horseshoes and Hand Grenades (5.12a)

Seconds to Darkness (5.8)

New Tricks for Old Dogs (5.10a)

Climbing El Capitan

Many people, upon arriving in Yosemite, are bowled over by the vast array of experiences the park offers. Do you want to spend your day in skis, climbing shoes, or slippers? Do you want to see waterfalls, glaciers, or John Muir? Was that bird a junco, a raven, or a golden eagle? Where to stay? What to eat? How much to spend? You don't need to climb atop Yosemite's mountains and ask a guru in a cave. Along with its many choices, Yosemite offers many places to learn about the park and shape your experience into what you want it to be. The best place to start (of course) is the book in your hand, but if you want to delve deeper or learn more, here is a list of places to look.

Curry Village (Yosemite Valley)

The Curry Village Store (books, guides, maps)

The Yosemite Mountain Shop (historic displays, advice)

Occasional presentations at Curry Village

Sierra Club presentations at the LeConte Memorial Lodge

Nature Center at Happy Isles (books, exhibits)

Yosemite Village (Yosemite Valley)

The Yosemite Village Store (books, maps, DVDs)

Wawona Visitor Center at Hill's Studio

The Wilderness Center (exhibits, maps, advice)

The Ansel Adams Gallery (books, all things photographic)

The Visitor Center (advice, forecasts, many exhibits)

The Yosemite Bookstore (books on all things remotely related to Yosemite)

The Yosemite Museum and its rotating special exhibits (books, exhibits, and presentations focusing on all things about Indians in Yosemite)

The Yosemite Theater, featuring *Spirit of Yosemite* (an excellent short film about Yosemite)

Presentations at the Yosemite Lodge

Wawona/Mariposa Grove

Mariposa Grove Gift Shop (advice, books)

The Wawona Store (books, advice)

The Wawona Museum (historic exhibits)

The Wawona Visitor Center (advice, forecasts, maps)

Glacier Point

The Glacier Point Store (books, advice)

Ranger presentations at Glacier Point

Big Oak Flat

The Big Oak Flat Information Station (Books, maps, forecasts, advice)

The Crane Flat gas station store (books)

Tioga Road

The Tuolumne Mountain Shop (books, advice)

Ranger presentations at the Tuolumne campground

Presentations at Parsons Memorial Lodge

The Tuolumne Visitor Center (books, forecasts, advice)

Wilderness Center (maps, forecasts, advice)

Many gift shops, coffee shops, gas stations, and restaurants in communities surrounding the park have information of all kinds, from maps to guest speakers.

And there are many, many interpretive signs all over the whole darn place.

Many tourists go to Yosemite hoping to get away. For those who don't, or can't, don't worry. If you need Internet or cell phone reception, you will eventually find it in the park. To ease your search for a signal, here are some tips.

Cell Phone Coverage

The cell coverage described here is for Verizon (via Golden State Cellular). AT&T has limited or no service in Wawona, El Portal, or Yosemite West. Your best bet for coverage remains Yosemite Valley. You will hit occasional dead spots, but in general coverage is pretty solid, especially in the heavily trafficked east end of the valley. The signal may fade if you're too close to one of the valley's walls. Above the walls, on Glacier Point and Sentinel Dome, you should be able to get service. Please be aware of other hikers if you talk on your cell phone on the trail.

With some carriers there is some reception in other areas. The signal in El Portal, in the Merced Canyon, is a little uneven, but Foresta, 2,000 feet higher, is pretty well covered. Yosemite West has very limited reception, but there's enough that it's worth a try if you need to make or take a call. Fish Camp, south of Yosemite, has patchy reception that improves as you go higher up. There is a little reception in Wawona, in the area surrounding the Wawona Hotel. Along Tioga Road, Crane Flat has decent reception, but then you have to wait until you reach Tuolumne Meadows before coverage picks up again.

Generally speaking, coverage improves as you go farther up or farther west, out of the canyons. A small rise can make a big difference.

Do not rely on your cell phone while hiking. There is very little coverage in the backcountry. As NPS ranger Brad Benter says, a cell phone is not a first aid kit. Don't put yourself into a risky situation and assume that you can phone for help and get out of trouble. If you decide to go somewhere dangerous, in the high country or in Yosemite's canyons, make sure that your party has the necessary skill and supplies to deal with emergencies.

Using your phone while driving in Yosemite is a terrible idea. There are simply no stretches of highway that are straight and have consistent reception. Contending with RVs, tour buses, weather, and wildlife is enough of a challenge on Yosemite's narrow, winding roads without trying to put in your earpiece (as required by California law) and hold a patchy conversation. Your call can wait.

The Internet

Public Internet access is limited in Yosemite National Park. There are a few places where wireless Internet is available to the public, most notably at Yosemite Lodge. The public can settle in at the bar and work on their laptops.

The public libraries of Wawona, Yosemite Valley, and El Portal offer public Internet access. Each spot has variable hours that are dependent on the season and the day. Schedules can be found on the Mariposa County library website, www.mariposalibrary.org.

The larger gateway towns on routes 41, 140, and 120 have coffee shops with wireless Internet access. There's a charge for wireless Internet access in Oakhurst and Mariposa, but Groveland's Mountain Sage features free wireless along with its many other charms.

Early tourists in Yosemite Valley, c. 1900

2 | Yosemite History

The recorded history of Yosemite National Park is as fascinating and important as it is short relative to that of other parts of the US and the world. While Native Americans were long-term residents, European Americans did not enter Yosemite Valley until 1851 and did not occupy it in any meaningful way until the 1860s. Yet Yosemite's history over the past century and a half is particularly significant, because the actions of both people and governments here have pioneered conservation efforts on behalf of natural areas all around the globe. There is little question that at Yosemite the concept of national parks was born, and the park still serves as a model and symbol for the entire world.

People resided in the Yosemite region for about eight thousand years before Spain occupied California. Anthropologists suggest that the earliest inhabitants came from the east side of the Sierra Nevada looking for water and food in particularly dry years. Later, as populations increased and competition for homelands grew, groups from the Central Valley (predominantly Miwok-speaking) moved into the foothills and greater Yosemite. These groups merged and established permanent villages near the Merced River throughout Yosemite Valley.

There is no recorded history of native peoples in Yosemite until very recent times. Anthropologists believe that the culture evolved very slowly: a simple lifestyle involving seed and plant gathering, hunting, and trade remained relatively unchanged, no doubt, for centuries. Yosemite's Native Americans spent fall and winter in the valley or the warmer foothills, then roamed into the high country in spring and summer in quest of food and to barter with Mono Lake Paiutes and other people from east of the area.

The first Europeans that native Californians came into contact with were Spanish missionaries, soldiers, and settlers in the eighteenth century. As more and more Europeans settled in the central and southern parts of the state, white encroachment on traditional Indian territory increased. Some people believe that at the beginning of the 1800s the Indian people of Yosemite were

A Native American family in Yosemite, c. 1900

struck with a "fatal black sickness," a plague of some type. Reportedly, the few survivors abandoned the valley and relocated to the eastern Sierra and were assimilated by other groups there. For a number of years (the exact number unknown), Yosemite Valley may have been uninhabited.

One of the Yosemite people who grew up with the Mono Paiutes was Tenaya (see page 50). As a youth, Tenaya heard stories of the beauty and bounty of Yosemite Valley. He finally visited the former home of his people quite late in his life. Being favorably impressed, he and two hundred others (some Yosemite descendants, some not) resettled the valley. Tenaya was named chief of the group.

These people lived in relative harmony in the valley they called "Ah-wah-nee" until the gold rush and the fateful Euro-American occupation of the Sierra foothills began in 1849. Ahwahnee (as it is spelled now) probably means "place of a gaping mouth," although Lafayette Bunnell of the Mariposa Battalion reported that through hand signals the native people had indicated its meaning was "deep, grassy valley."

As friction between gold seekers and foothill Indians increased, anti-Indian sentiments blossomed. Groups native to the Central Valley moved higher into the foothills, and conflict resulted between rival Native American groups as well as between whites and native people. As Tenaya and his fellows defiantly protected their mountain stronghold, the Mariposa Battalion was formed to locate and capture the native residents and relocate them to reservations. The members of the Mariposa Battalion were the first white people in the Yosemite Valley. Soon "Ahwahnee" became "Yosemite." The natives called themselves the Ahwahneechees. The white soldiers called them the "Yosemites." Some say this came from the Miwok word "uzumati," or grizzly bear. The origin that is now considered correct is that it is a corruption of the word "Yoche-ma-te," which means "some among them are killers." Whatever the word's meaning, it is true that the local Indians were known as fierce fighters and that they lived in an area where grizzly bears were fairly common.

Following Tenaya's death in 1853, what was left of the band of Yosemite Indians dispersed. Some went east to the Mono Lake area, while others joined neighboring peoples along the Tuolumne River. Never again did the remaining Yosemites gather together as a people.

Within twenty years, the number of Native Americans living in the Yosemite area dwindled to below fifty. With white settlement of Yosemite Valley and ever-increasing tourism, the native culture was irrevocably corrupted. Hotelkeepers and other concessioners employed some of the Ahwahneechees for odd jobs and manual labor, but the truth is that they were only tolerated at best.

A Gentle Lifestyle

During their hundreds of years of life in Yosemite Valley, the native people of Yosemite were remarkably gentle in their use of the land. There were at least forty different camp spots on the floor of the valley. Most of them were summer encampments only. Because of heavy snow and extremely cold temperatures, the bulk of the valley residents moved to the El Portal area and the foothills below to pass the severe winter months.

The typical house was a conical lean-to covered with three layers of cedar bark slabs, affording reasonable shelter from the elements. There were also earth-covered dance houses and sweathouses, and small elevated granaries for storing acorns and other edibles.

The staple of the Native American diet in Yosemite and much of the rest of California was acorn, which was painstakingly prepared and eaten as mush. Mushrooms as well as ferns, clover, bulbs, and other plant foods were also eaten. Fish and game included deer, squirrels, rabbits, trout, and the Sacramento sucker. Some insects, like certain fly pupae, caterpillars, and grasshoppers were considered delicacies.

Native people in Yosemite wove fairly coarse twined baskets and finer coiled baskets with elaborate patterns, as well as cradles. They also made bows and arrows, obsidian tools and implements, bone awls and scrapers, and ceremonial costumes.

Today Native Americans play an important part in the cultural preservation and interpretation of Yosemite Miwok/Paiute sites in the park. Be sure to visit the Yosemite Museum, where expert interpreters demonstrate traditional native skills.

Basket Culture

Yosemite's Native Americans were part of a trading network that extended from the desert east of the mountains to the Pacific coast. In return for shells, obsidian, and other goods, they offered their finely woven baskets. Many people in the twenty-first century don't recognize the value of

A handmade Native American basket

these baskets, but for native Californians, baskets were the only way to contain or transport many things, from food to trade goods to babies.

Through the arrival of Europeans and the destruction of native culture, basketry survived. Part of this was a matter of utility—native people use baskets for cooking, carrying, and gathering to this day. Some baskets are so watertight and sturdy that they can be used to boil water with the use of heated rocks, a necessity for cooking acorns. For the tourists flocking to Yosemite, though, baskets came to represent local Native American culture, and fine baskets are now worth thousands of dollars. Tourists presented an opportunity for the Miwok/Paiute women living in the valley to demonstrate their skills for the rest of the world, and to supplement their incomes. Basketry takes work, though—large baskets like those found in the Yosemite Museum can take three to four years to create.

The skills of collecting and preparing materials and then forming these materials into baskets have been passed down from generation to generation since the earliest times. In Yosemite, these skills live today in Julia Parker, who learned how to weave from her mother-in-law, famed Miwok weaver Lucy Telles. Parker's ancestry is Coast Miwok and Kashaya Pomo, but she has lived in Yosemite since she was seventeen and has demonstrated basketry to Yosemite visitors for more than fifty years. She has taught traditional basketry to thousands of people, including her daughter, granddaughter, and great-granddaughter, and she can often be found in the Yosemite Museum, surrounded by visitors, explaining and demonstrating native skills and culture while hard at work on her latest basket.

Yosemite Valley was sighted by Euro-Americans for the first time in 1833. A party of explorers headed by Joseph R. Walker was crossing the Sierra Nevada that fall, and in their efforts to determine the best route, several of the group came upon the north rim of the valley. The cliffs were described as "more than a mile high," and after several efforts the mountaineers determined that they were "utterly impossible for a man to descend, to say nothing of our horses."

Yosemite Falls by artist Thomas Ayres

It was not until twenty years later that non-natives first entered Yosemite Valley.

In response to actions by the Yosemite Indians and their neighbors in defense of their homeland, a group of men was organized as the Mariposa Battalion to kill Indians as they deemed necessary and to transport survivors to reservations in the Central Valley. A punitive expedition was mounted in March of 1851, and their quest for Indians led the battalion into Yosemite Valley, where they beheld what no other group of pioneers had seen before.

It wasn't long before the word began to spread about Yosemite's wonders. Letters from members of the Mariposa Battalion to San Francisco newspapers aroused the interest of James Mason Hutchings, who organized the first tourist party to Yosemite Valley in 1855. He brought the artist Thomas Ayres to sketch the region's geologic features and used the sketches to disseminate Yosemite's fame even more widely.

An ever-increasing stream of visitors arrived primarily on foot and horseback, but as the years passed, wagon roads were developed to permit yet greater visitation.

Hutchings became the chief entrepreneur and publicist for Yosemite, homesteading land and operating a hotel. Other hotels and residences were built, livestock was grazed in the meadows, crops were planted, orchards were established, and Yosemite Valley was treated as no more than a resource to be exploited.

The State Grant

Fortunately, not everyone viewed the valley as a capitalist's dream come true. Some amazingly farsighted persons took it upon themselves to work for the protection of Yosemite Valley for the public good. These early-day conservationists, I. W. Raymond and Frederick Law Olmsted (the landscape architect who, with Calvert Vaux, designed New York's Central Park) prominent among them, appealed to Congress. Senator John Conness introduced a bill to grant Yosemite Valley and the Mariposa Grove of Big Trees to the State of California for preservation and protection. The bill was passed, and in the midst of the Civil War President Abraham Lincoln signed the legislation, on June 30, 1864.

It was a landmark event. Never before had a government set aside a piece of land for its inherent natural and scenic qualities to be preserved for public use, resort, and recreation "inalienable for all time." Yosemite became, in effect, the first state park and the first national park in the world. It unquestionably served as a model for the development of other parks and led to the birth of the national park system as we know it in the US today.

Public Management

Responsibility for management of the Yosemite Grant (as it came to be called) fell to a Board of Commissioners appointed by California's governor and to the "Guardian" that the board hired.

Yosemite's first guardian was Galen Clark (see page 50).

The 1860s and 1870s saw improved access to the valley thanks to the completion of several wagon roads, and the guardian had to contend with an astounding increase in the number of visitors.

Many new hostelries were built, including the extravagant Cosmopolitan Bathhouse and Saloon, Black's Hotel, Leidig's Hotel, La Casa Nevada Hotel, the Stoneman House, and others. Competition was fierce among the various operators, and unsuspecting visitors found themselves heavily lobbied by concessioners seeking their business.

Despite the much-publicized scenery, things in Yosemite were far from peaceful and quiet. Given the intense public interest in Yosemite as well as the disappointment of the original settlers, who saw their opportunities to make a killing disappear, Yosemite politics were never boring. Several lawsuits were brought by individuals who were dispossessed by the Yosemite Grant (Hutchings foremost among them), and criticism was regularly leveled at the Board of Commissioners.

Clark's Station, 1866

Greater Yosemite

While Yosemite Valley and the Mariposa Grove had been recognized and protected, the thousands of acres of wilderness surrounding these relatively small park strongholds had not. Led by John Muir (see page 51) and by easterner Robert Underwood Johnson (editor of the then-influential *Century Magazine*), a group of preservationists began to focus attention on the need to protect the greater Yosemite area, including the beautiful high-country regions, such as Tuolumne Meadows.

As resource degradation in the form of mining, logging, and stock grazing increased, so did the efforts of Yosemite champions. Muir and Johnson did their best to influence Congress and to inform the American people about the threats to Yosemite. They derived important support from the Southern Pacific Railroad and its president, Edward Harriman, who were strongly interested in boosting tourism in the Sierra Nevada.

On October 1, 1890, the US government acknowledged the preciousness of these wildlands by enacting the law that established Yosemite National Park. Interestingly, Yosemite National Park did not include Yosemite Valley or the Mariposa Grove, but encompassed an enormous area around them. The park was actually 30 percent larger than it is today.

Early tourists, c. 1880s

The brand new national park needed management, and in 1890, the National Park Service had not yet been established. It was determined that the US Army would assume the administration of Yosemite, and members of the cavalry became a common sight in the park. Because a deep blanket of snow covered much of the area during the winter months, the Army limited its occupation of Yosemite to summers only. Usually soldiers from San Francisco would ride or march to and from their headquarters in Wawona each summer.

The duties of the cavalrymen were multiple and varied. They chased sheepherders from high-country meadows, explored previously uncharted regions of the park, blazed trails, surveyed boundaries, prepared maps, and prevented poachers from illegally taking park game. The work done by Army personnel was prodigious, and their mark on Yosemite's history was a major one.

During the Spanish-American War, when many US troops were engaged, civilian rangers were hired by the Army to assist at the park. They were the first of their kind.

The existence of two different administrations, one for Yosemite Valley and the Mariposa Grove of Big Trees, the other for the greater Yosemite National Park, inevitably led to duplication, overlap, and conflict. Many individuals and organizations (including John Muir and the Sierra Club) began to push for a unification of all of Yosemite under the management of one entity.

A Single Yosemite

The mood of the public was apparently shared by lawmakers and government officials. In 1906 the federal government formally accepted the "recession" of Yosemite Valley and the Mariposa Grove from the State of California, an action that obviated the Yosemite Grant once and for all. The price of the agreement was the reduction in overall size of the park to conform it to natural boundaries and to exclude private mining and timber holdings. But at last there was one Yosemite National Park with a single administration.

The US Army continued its management of the park, moving its headquarters to Yosemite Valley (to a site near the present-day Yosemite Lodge). In 1914 a civilian administration was established, with the Department of the Interior authorizing and employing park rangers.

Troop F on the Fallen Monarch, 1899

Buffalo Soldiers, the 24th Mounted Infantry

The years between 1890 and 1914 were characterized by a transportation revolution. Regular stage lines began operation, and private wagons commonly made the trip to Yosemite. The remarkable increase in visitation continued, and then the completion of the Yosemite Valley Railroad from Merced to El Portal in 1907 effectively heralded the end of the stage era in Yosemite. But more earthshaking changes in transportation were still to come.

It was in 1900 that the automobile first entered Yosemite Valley (albeit illegally). The US Army officially allowed automobiles into the park in 1913, and when they came, they came with a vengeance. Two years later, all horse-drawn stages connecting train passengers to Yosemite Valley were replaced by motor stages. By 1920, two-thirds of all visitors were coming to Yosemite via private automobile.

The period also witnessed growth and proliferation of concessioner facilities. Public campgrounds were initiated, Camp Curry was established, Best's Studio was founded, and Camp Ahwahnee was built at the base of Sentinel Rock. Competition remained hot and heavy, and considerable conflict resulted between concessioners.

A regrettable chapter in Yosemite's history was written during the Army years. The famous and bitter battle over the damming of the Hetch Hetchy Valley was settled in 1913 with the enactment of the Raker Act and the resulting inundation of the area. See page 125 for more about the Hetch Hetchy controversy.

Buffalo Soldiers

When tourists arrived in Yosemite between 1891 and 1914, they would be greeted by soldiers wearing the blue uniforms and gold braid familiar to everyone who's seen a Western movie. A surprise to some of the tourists then and many researchers now is that several of the units that guarded Yosemite were made up of black men—the famous Buffalo Soldiers. During that era, black cavalry and infantry (under the command of white officers, as dictated by Army policy) built roads, blazed trails, fought fires, and guarded mountains. Unfortunately, the stories of these men have been lost, overlooked even by Yosemite historians, who have focused on the stories of Galen Clark, John Muir, and the Firefall. But soldiers, black and white, played a pivotal role in the story of the national parks. In an era when the dominant approach to land in America was to make as much money out of it as possible, the Army kept out herders and poachers, enforcing the law and preserving the park (as the modern Park Service's mission statement has it) for the "enjoyment, education, and inspiration of this and future generations." The experience of patrolling Yosemite's meadows and canyons, and the authority that came with their positions, provided the Buffalo Soldiers with opportunities that were denied them in most of America. Like many people, these long-ago Americans came to Yosemite and found a freedom like none they'd ever known.

A Yosemite Chronology

1833—Yosemite Valley was first seen by Euro-Americans. Crossing the Sierra, the Joseph Walker party encountered a valley with "precipices more than a mile high" that were "impossible for a man to descend."

1851—The Mariposa Battalion, under the command of Major James Savage, became the first group of pioneers to enter Yosemite Valley. They were pursuing "intransigent" Indians.

1852—The Mariposa Grove of Big Trees was discovered by a party of prospectors.

1855—The first tourist party visited Yosemite Valley, with James Mason Hutchings as guide. Thomas Ayres, an artist with the group, made the first known sketches of Yosemite Valley.

1856—The first permanent structure, the Lower Hotel, was built in Yosemite Valley at the base of Sentinel Rock. The first trail into Yosemite Valley was completed by Milton and Houston Mann.

1859—The first photograph in Yosemite Valley was made by C. L. Weed. His subject was the Upper Hotel.

1864—Yosemite Valley and the Mariposa Grove of Big Trees were set aside by the federal government as the world's first state park. Florence Hutchings was the first white child to be born in Yosemite Valley.

1866—Galen Clark was named the first Yosemite guardian.

1868—John Muir made his first trip to Yosemite.

1871—The first ascent of Mt. Lyell, Yosemite's highest peak, was accomplished by J. B. Tileston on August 29.

1874—The first road into Yosemite Valley, the Coulterville Road, was completed. The Big Oak Flat Road was finished a month later.

1875—George Anderson made the first ascent of Half Dome before the installation of ropes or cables. The first public school was opened in Yosemite Valley.

1878—The first public campgrounds in Yosemite Valley were opened by A. Harris near the site of the present-day Ahwahnee Hotel.

1890—Yosemite National Park was established. The park did not include Yosemite Valley or the Mariposa Grove of Big Trees, but it encompassed a large region around them.

1891—Telephones were installed in Yosemite Valley for the first time.

1892—The California Fish and Game Commission first planted trout in Yosemite waters.

1896—Firearms were prohibited from the park.

1898—The first civilian park ranger, Archie Leonard, was employed at Yosemite.

1900—Oliver Lippincott and Edward C. Russell drove the first automobile (a Locomobile) to enter Yosemite.

1903—President Theodore Roosevelt goes camping with John Muir in Yosemite for three days.

1907—The first railway line to Yosemite, the Yosemite Valley Railroad, began operation.

1913—Automobiles were officially admitted to Yosemite.

1915—The first appropriation for the construction of the John Muir Trail was approved.

1916—The National Park Service was established. Washington B. Lewis was named the first NPS superintendent at Yosemite.

1917—The first High Sierra Camp, Tuolumne Meadows Lodge, was installed.

1919—The first airplane in Yosemite Valley, piloted by Lt. J. S. Krull, landed on May 27.

1921—The first installations in the Yosemite Museum were completed.

1926—The Yosemite Museum opened to the public.

1934—Water from the Hetch Hetchy Reservoir first flowed into San Francisco.

1935—Badger Pass Ski Area was developed.

John Muir and Theodore Roosevelt at Glacier Point, 1903

1940—Ostrander Ski Hut was opened for winter use.

1946—The first ascent of the Lost Arrow Spire was accomplished by four climbers on September 2.

1949—The first use of a helicopter for rescue purposes in Yosemite was made at Benson Lake to fly an injured boy to safety.

1951—Trout were planted in Yosemite by airplane for the first time.

1954—Annual park visitation exceeded one million for the first time: 1,008,031 visitors were recorded.

1958—The first climb up the face of El Capitan was completed.

The historic Wells Fargo Office at the Yosemite Pioneer History Center

1961—Pioneer Yosemite History Center opened to the public.

1966—The new Yosemite Valley Visitor Center was built.

1967—For the first time, over two million visitors to Yosemite were recorded.

1969—The Firefall from Glacier Point was discontinued. The famed Wawona Tunnel Tree toppled over from the weight of its winter snow load.

1970—The free shuttle bus system was initiated in Yosemite Valley.

1972—The first asphalt was removed from the parking lot in front of the Yosemite Valley Visitor Center. The area was converted to use as a pedestrian mall.

1974—Hang gliding was officially allowed from Glacier Point, and 170 flights were made.

1976—Tioga Road opened on April 10, its earliest opening on record.

1980—The Yosemite General Management Plan, the park's first systematically developed, long-range planning document, was approved.

1981—Captive-born peregrine falcon chicks were successfully reared in a nest on El Capitan.

1983—Yosemite's first prescribed burn took place in the Mariposa Grove.

1984—Yosemite was added to the World Heritage List. The California Wilderness Bill designated 94 percent of the park as wilderness.

1986—California bighorn sheep were reintroduced into Yosemite.

1987—Annual park visitation exceeded three million for the first time: 3,266,342 visitors were recorded.

1990—Yosemite celebrated its 100th birthday as a national park. Major forest fires raked the park during August.

1992—Delaware North Company was awarded the Yosemite concession contract by the National Park Service.

1994—Annual park visitation exceeded four million visitors for the first time.

1995—The Yosemite Wilderness Center opened its doors, and the wilderness permit reservation system was initiated.

1996—A massive rockfall in Yosemite Valley downed several hundred trees, damaged the Happy Isles Nature Center, and killed one visitor.

1997—Due to major flooding in the valley, some 450 campsites, 350 motel and cabin units, and 200 concessioner housing units were lost. Estimated cost of repairs was $178 million. The valley was closed to visitors for three months.

1999—Camp Curry celebrated its 100th anniversary.

2001—New Homeland Security efforts tightened visitor access to Hetch Hetchy.

2006—Yosemite became a sister park to two National Parks in China: Huangshan and Jiuzhaigou.

2007—Yosemite became a sister park to Torres del Paine in Chile.

2008—A major rockfall hit several cabins in Curry Village, prompting the closure and removal of over 70 structures.

2009—Ken Burns's documentary *America's Best Idea: the National Parks* aired on public television.

2010—Yosemite National Park instituted a day-hiker permit system for Half Dome. The nonprofits Yosemite Association and Yosemite Fund reunited as Yosemite Conservancy.

2012—Tioga Road closed on January 17, the latest closing on record.

The National Park Service

A major change came about in the national park system with the creation of the National Park Service in 1916. It had been recognized that administration of the parks required more than the part-time attention of the Army and that there was a war to be fought in Europe. The National Park Service was the Interior Department's chosen alternative.

It was Frederick Law Olmsted Jr. (whose father had been influential in the establishment of the 1864 Yosemite Grant) who proposed that the new agency should "conserve the scenery and the natural and historic objects and the wildlife therein, and…provide for the enjoyment of the same in such manner and by such means as will leave them unimpaired for the enjoyment of future generations." This phrase became the cornerstone of the act that created the NPS and guides the agency still.

The years following 1916 were significant not only for Yosemite but also for all US national parks because the basic policies of the agency were being developed and implemented. The process of interpreting the NPS mandate to preserve the parks while allowing for their use was ongoing. Yosemite consistently was the park where new ideas were first tested and applied.

A nature walk early in the park's history, c. 1919

Yosemite's new National Park Service superintendent was Washington B. "Dusty" Lewis, who was responsible for many innovations and changes at the park. During his twelve-year tenure the concessions were consolidated under one principal operating company (The Yosemite Park & Curry Company), roads including the Tioga Road were improved and tolls eliminated, new accommodations were built in Yosemite Valley (Yosemite Lodge and the Ahwahnee Hotel) and at Glacier Point, a new administrative center was built, and utilities, roads, and buildings were modernized.

Interpretation

It was also shortly after the birth of the park service that Yosemite personnel inaugurated the educational program so familiar to park visitors today. The original program was the inspiration of Dr. C. M. Goethe, and Harold Bryant and Loye Miller were hired as Yosemite's first "nature guides" in 1920. At the outset the interpretive program was pretty much limited to nature walks, but it has evolved to include visitor center displays, campfire programs, informal talks, multimedia presentations, and informational literature.

A logical extension of the interpretive program was the Yosemite Museum, plans for which were hatched about 1921. Several years later a permanent museum was completed in the park, thanks to a gift from the Laura Spelman Rockefeller Memorial. At the same time a Field School of Natural History was established in Yosemite to provide for the training of future interpreters and nature guides.

These formative years of the NPS reflected the realization that protection of the parks depended on a strong program of education designed to increase public awareness of the special values embodied by Yosemite and other outstanding natural areas. The Yosemite model has been emulated throughout the world and is still as vital as it was ninety years ago.

The Modern Years

The past seventy-five years in Yosemite have seen consistent management and burgeoning visitation. With scientific research and experience, resource policies have changed. Fire is no longer viewed as evil, wild animals are managed to be wild, and artificial attractions like the Firefall from Glacier Point have been eliminated.

The greatest challenge facing Yosemite today is its popularity. With visitation hovering between three and four million people each year, the park sometimes suffers from overcrowding, congestion, and air pollution. Resources are degraded and the visitor's experience is diminished. It can only be hoped that the coming years will provide solutions to these thorny problems and that Yosemite will long remain the preeminent national park in the world.

The following locations have special historical significance or were the sites of early development in Yosemite Valley. They are listed in order of locale, beginning at the west end of the valley, continuing to the east along Southside Drive, focusing on the east end of Yosemite Valley, and then heading back to the west along Northside Drive. In your explorations, remember that all cultural resources should be left unimpaired, and that digging and the use of metal detectors are not allowed.

Bridalveil Meadow

About a half mile before the Wawona/ Highway 41 turnoff

This spot is where the Mariposa Battalion camped in March 1851. The party was in search of Indians and was the first group of whites ever to enter Yosemite Valley. Around a campfire here, the group proposed and applied the name "Yo-sem-ite" to this marvel of nature's handiwork. It was also here that President Theodore Roosevelt and John Muir camped in 1903 and discussed the need to preserve our nation's wilderness areas.

Bridalveil Fall

Just past the turnoff for Wawona

This is roughly the place where the wagon road from Wawona entered Yosemite Valley. Towards the Merced River through the trees, a large sewer plant operated for many years. The sewer plant was removed in 1987, and over three acres were freed of development. Yosemite Valley sewage is now carried by pipeline to a new processing facility in El Portal.

El Capitan View

Look for the long straightaway with El Capitan towering to the right

Just upriver from here is the site of the bear-feeding platform used in the 1920s and 1930s. Garbage was dumped on the lighted platform, drawing bears and gawking tourists each night. Enlightened managers have long since dispensed with the spectacle.

El Capitan meadow

Sentinel Rock View

Immediately past the Sentinel Beach picnic turnoff on Southside Drive

Here was a portion of Lower Yosemite Village, which included the Yosemite Chapel (later moved to its present location east of here); Leidig's Hotel, which operated from 1869 to 1888; and Camp Ahwahnee (1908–1915). This is also the trailhead for James McCauley's Four-Mile Trail to Glacier Point, where for several years a tollhouse was maintained to collect fees from hikers and horseback riders. Some locust trees are the only visible remnants of this earlier occupation.

Swinging Bridge Turnout

The turnout is about a quarter mile past the Sentinel Rock View on the left

The remainder of Lower Yosemite Village was located here. Black's Hotel stood from 1869 through 1888. Photographer George Fiske's residence and studio were near the river to the west. Galen Clark had a residence here. The Coffman & Kenney Stables operated for several years. A boardwalk nearly a half-mile in length was constructed through the meadow to the east to connect the Upper and Lower Village areas.

Chapel Parking Area

About one-half mile beyond Swinging Bridge on the right

This area was covered by extensive development from the 1860s until the 1950s. Here were the Upper Hotel (known at various times as Hutchings House, the Sentinel Hotel, and the Yosemite Falls Hotel); photographic studios (Boysen's, Foley's, and Pillsbury's); Best's Studio; Degnan's Store and Restaurant; the world-famous Cosmopolitan Bathhouse and Saloon; the Village Store; and many other structures. In 1925 the "new" Yosemite Village site (the present location) was selected, and an administration building, museum, post office, and several artist studios were built. Slowly the Upper (old) Village was dismantled and razed. The Village Store was the last major building to go, in 1959. The observant historian can still find plenty of evidence of Yosemite's yesteryears with a little exploring here.

Yosemite Chapel in Yosemite Valley

Stoneman Meadow

Near Curry Village

This meadow has been the center of much activity over the years. Within it stood a large wooden hotel called the Stoneman House, built by the state of California in 1886, that burned in 1896. James Lamon, a settler in the park's earliest days, built a cabin near here and planted two apple orchards in 1859. One now serves as the Curry Village parking lot, and the other is behind the Valley Stable (shuttle bus stop 18). Stoneman Meadow will also be remembered as the site of a riot in 1970 which pitted young people against NPS personnel in a clash over curfews, noise levels, and lifestyles.

The Ahwahnee Hotel

Shuttle bus stop 3

Before the present hotel was built, an active stable business was operated at this spot. Known as Kenneyville, the stable was extensive and there were horses, shops, barns, and houses mingled here. When automobile travel became popular, the need for such a large stable was eliminated. In 1926, to make way for the Ahwahnee, the stable was moved to its present location and the old buildings torn down. Many people are unaware that during World War II between 1943 and 1945 the Ahwahnee Hotel was closed to the public and converted to use as a Naval Convalescent Hospital. During that time almost 7,000 patients were rehabilitated.

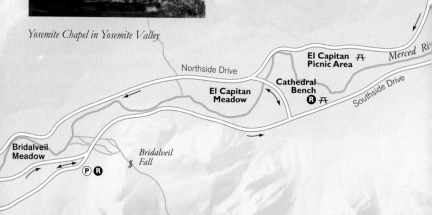

Yosemite Cemetery

Just west of and across the street from the Yosemite Museum, in Yosemite Village

This is the cemetery where local residents were buried between the 1870s and the 1950s. There's a wide variety of personalities interred here, from Indian Lucy, Sally Ann Castagnetto, and other Native Americans to such pioneer settlers and innkeepers as Galen Clark and James Mason Hutchings. A guide to the cemetery is for sale in the Visitor Center.

Yosemite Falls

Just west of Yosemite Village, near shuttle bus stop 6

In the forested area between the restrooms and Lower Yosemite Fall, James Mason Hutchings built a sawmill for preparation of lumber to upgrade his hotel. John Muir was employed to run the sawmill for a time and constructed a cabin for himself nearby. It featured running water: one strand of Yosemite Creek flowed right through it. Camp Yosemite, also known as Camp Lost Arrow, stood near the base of the fall and to its east from 1901 to 1915.

Yosemite Lodge

Shuttle bus stops 7 and 8

The lodge area was first developed as Army headquarters for the park in 1906. The facility included two large barracks buildings, two bathhouses and lavatories, 156 tent frames, and a parade ground. When the Army administration ended in 1914, so did the need for the headquarters, and they were converted to accommodate visitors in 1915.

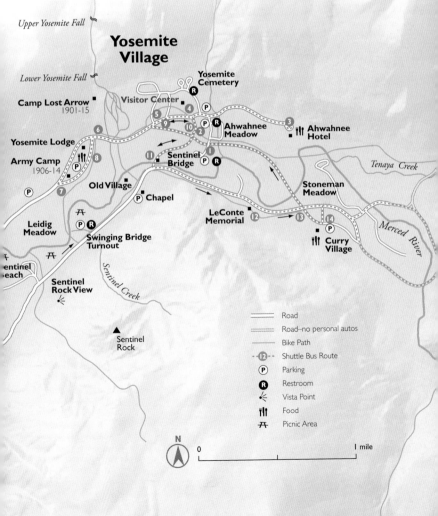

For at least thirty years, National Park Service managers worked to develop a plan to guide Yosemite's development in the coming century. In 1980 the "General Management Plan" was issued and approved.

The Yosemite Plan begins to address Yosemite's continuing challenges. Crowding three or four million people a year into Yosemite Valley, a space only about eight miles long by one and a half miles wide, is hard on the land, the facilities, the rangers, and the visitors themselves. Campfires fill the valley with haze visible even on sunny days. Sensitive or previously degraded areas of Yosemite Valley have been fenced off, but there is only so much of the valley that can be protected that way. Valley animals have grown so used to humans that they are no longer afraid of us. This is merely annoying in the case of squirrels, but potentially (though rarely) dangerous in the case of deer and bears. Should Yosemite be open to as many people as want to come? What if it gets five million? Ten million? Should it cut off the number of visitors each day? What should that cutoff be?

With people come cars. One of the unfortunate features of Yosemite Valley is the traffic jams that sometimes clog the roads, especially on summer weekends. Plans have been proposed to restrict the use of automobiles in Yosemite Valley, but so far they have had limited effects.

Development in Yosemite is an issue as well. Even paradise needs a parking lot. It also needs campsites, hotels, visitor centers, ranger offices, and all the other human aspects of a national park. But where to put them? If buildings go in too close to the river, they will be in the flood plain. If they go too close to the walls, they will be in the rockfall zone. There is precious little space between these two danger areas.

Yosemite does not exist in a vacuum. Outside developments carry over to the park itself. What effect will growth in the foothills, road construction, logging, hunting, pollution from the Central Valley, and many other trends have on Yosemite's future? At present the answers are debatable and the facts sketchy. One suggestion is to have a regional agency study these ongoing issues. Whether this will happen is up in the air.

Key Questions for Yosemite's Future

- As the population of the Central Valley of California continues to grow, how will park managers contend with four to five million people living within a two-hour drive of Yosemite?

- Should the National Park Service limit the total number of visitors to Yosemite to ensure the quality of each visitor's experience? Is the appropriate number four million, six million, eight million, or more?

- Will a regional agency ever be put in place to monitor the effects on Yosemite of road construction, logging, suburbanization, global climate change, acid and nutrient rain, and other impacts that originate outside the park?

- Should and will the National Park Service eliminate motor vehicle use in Yosemite?

Yosemite's Original Management Plan

When Yosemite Valley and the Mariposa Grove were set aside as a public reserve by the federal government in 1864, the State of California was charged with creating a commission to administer the new grant. Noted landscape architect Frederick Law Olmsted was delegated the job of preparing a report and setting out the policy that should guide the management of the grant.

Olmsted's management plan was a visionary document. Among his key points was that "The first requirement is to preserve the natural scenery and restrict within the narrowest limits the necessary accommodation of visitors." In elaborating, he stated, "Structures should not detract from the dignity of the scene. In preventing the sacrifice of anything that should be of the slightest value to visitors to the convenience, bad taste, playfulness, carelessness, or wanton destructiveness of present visitors, would probably yield in each case the interest of uncounted millions to the selfishness of a few."

When Yosemite's management plan is finally implemented, it will be interesting to see whether Olmsted's recommendations have been heeded.

Yosemite in Fiction

Since people started writing about it in the 1850s, Yosemite has figured as a grand locale for fiction. From mass-appeal romances to beatnik epics, the array is impressive. Following are some of the better or more unusual literary works set in Yosemite.

The Forge of God

This science fiction novel by Greg Bear (New York: Tom Doherty Associates, (1987) is set in "futuristic" 1997, when profound changes to the solar system threaten Earth with destruction. People migrate to Yosemite to await their imminent demise. The book climaxes with a cataclysm that yields a great description of the collapse of the Royal Arches, the blockage of Yosemite Falls, the burial of Curry Village, and the destruction of Half Dome.

Star Trek V: The Final Frontier

This book by J. M. Dillard (New York: Pocket Books, 1989) is a media spin-off in reverse. It grew out of the movie by the same title, part of which was filmed in the park. At one point, Captain Kirk attempts a free climb of El Capitan and falls to his apparent doom, only to have Spock (wearing levitation boots) catch him by the ankles in midair.

The Dharma Bums

The beat generation goes hiking! Here is Jack Kerouac's classic account of a 1955 climb of Yosemite's Matterhorn Peak (New York: Viking Press, 1958) by Kerouac, Gary Snyder, and John Montgomery, written as fiction. The description of two crazed beatniks bounding down the side of the Matterhorn, yodeling and laughing, is particularly joyful.

The Affair of the Jade Monkey

Detective Huntoon Rogers tracks a suspicious character to Yosemite in this mystery by Clifford Knight (1943; reprint 1993, Yosemite Association). A body is found, and then a hiker is murdered and a small jade monkey appears in another's pack. Can Huntoon solve the case and thwart an enemy plot against the nation?

Angels of Light

Jeffrey B. Long's Yosemite climbing novel with a twist (New York: William Morrow, 1987) is based loosely on the true story of the drug plane that crashed at Lower Merced Pass Lake in the park's backcountry.

Before the rangers caught on, hundreds of pounds of marijuana were packed out by Yosemite climbers. The author characterizes it as the end of innocence for the park's climbing subculture.

Images on Silver

Believe it or not, a Harlequin Romance set in Yosemite. In this novel by Rayanne Moore (Toronto: Harlequin Books, 1984), highly acclaimed wildlife photographer Christy Reilly meets Ranger Travis Jeffords. Travis keeps asking Christy why she has worked alone for so long. Christy's secret is something no man can understand.

Fires of Innocence

A steamy novel by Jane Bonander (New York: St. Martin's, 1994) set in the 1860s. In a snowbound cabin, Alex Golovin, a government attorney bent on buying up land for the national park, and Scotty MacDowell, daughter of a valley homesteader, come to know each other. Thrilling her with "searing kisses and teasing caresses," he will not let the "sensuous spitfire" stand in the way of his work.

Nurse in Yosemite

Nurse Doralee Dahlquist moves to Yosemite and takes a job at the medical clinic in this novel by Beatrice Warren (New York: Avalon Books, 1982). All goes well until she falls for photographer Angus McGonigal. The conflict arises with fellow nurse Jan Stagnetto's claim that she will marry handsome Angus. Will Angus resist Jan's charms or will Doralee get dumped?

A Body to Dye For

This one's about a gay hairdresser/detective who finds the dead body of a Yosemite park ranger in the bed of one of his regular customers. With a colorful cast of characters, author Grant Michaels (New York: St. Martin's Press, 1990) details the detective's efforts to solve the case by following leads back to Yosemite.

High Sierra

Famed national park mystery writer Nevada Barr finally inserts her protagonist Anna Pigeon into Yosemite (New York: Putnam & Sons, 2004). She's working undercover as a waitress at the Ahwahnee, where her coworkers' odd behavior leads her into a backcountry showdown with some evil druggies: Yosemite as the dark side.

The Yosemite Hall of Fame

Chief Tenaya

Chief Tenaya, leader of the native people in Yosemite when Euro-Americans first arrived in the valley, in 1851, has been called not only a brave warrior but an unusual personality who commanded the respect of his people.

Accounts have it that a tribal shaman warned Tenaya that "horsemen of the lowlands" (probably a reference to the Spaniards) represented the gravest threat to his people and should be guarded against. When in 1849 gold miners began entering the foothills and interacting with the native residents, Tenaya apparently felt threatened. He reportedly informed the invading whites that his people would be peaceable, but only if they could continue to occupy Yosemite Valley and not be disturbed.

This arrangement was unacceptable to the new foothill residents. The Mariposa Battalion was dispatched to subdue Yosemite's native people and in May 1851 the greatest portion of the band was rounded up and marched to a reservation in the Central Valley. Problems arose, the federal government never ratified a treaty, and by the end of the year, Tenaya and his people had either escaped or been permitted to return to Yosemite Valley.

The following year, Native Americans in the valley allegedly attacked a party of miners, and further efforts to remove them resulted. Tenaya's group fled to the high country of Yosemite and to the east side again. In 1853 they returned once more to Yosemite Valley, but their fate was practically sealed.

Despite his best efforts, Tenaya was unable to protect his people and their homeland from the incursions of the whites. He was killed by stoning late in 1853. There are two versions of his death; the more commonly accepted one is that the Yosemite Indians stole horses from their eastern Sierran neighbors, who attacked in retribution.

Tenaya's name is common in the park today, having been attached to a canyon, a lake, and other features.

Galen Clark

Known as the "Guardian of Yosemite," Galen Clark was as intimately involved in Yosemite's early history as any other person. He moved to the park in 1856 at the age of forty-two, suffering from a debilitating lung disease that doctors had said would quickly end his life. The Yosemite fresh air and inspiring scenery must have been therapeutic; Clark lived to be ninety-five.

He first settled in Wawona, developing his place as a stopping point on the stage route to Yosemite (Clark's Station). He visited the Mariposa Grove of Big Trees in 1857 with Milton Mann, then explored the trees and publicized them. He recognized the value and uniqueness of the sequoias and Yosemite Valley, and he worked to bring about the enactment of the 1864 law that set aside the Yosemite Valley and Mariposa Big Trees as the world's first state park.

In 1866 Clark became the first "Yosemite Guardian," employed by the State of California to oversee the grant. He continued in this job until the political winds changed in 1880 and a new guardian was employed. He worked odd jobs for nine years and then was hired once again to be the guardian. His second term lasted seven years, and he closed out his life by guiding, writing books about the park, and helping wherever he could.

As guardian, Clark made many needed improvements, worked to relocate homesteaders, and persevered in his efforts to protect Yosemite. John Muir called him "the best mountaineer I ever met…one of the most sincere tree-lovers I ever knew." Following his death, Clark was buried in the Yosemite Cemetery in a grave shaded by sequoias he had planted and headed by a granite marker upon which he had chiseled his name.

James Mason Hutchings

James Hutchings will be remembered most for being Yosemite's first and best publicist. A native of England, in 1855 he organized and led the first "tourist" party to visit the valley, bringing with him the artist Thomas Ayres, who sketched Yosemite's wonders. Hutchings published the sketches and paired them with his descriptions of the place, drawing national attention to a previously unknown scenic treasure.

Like Galen Clark, when his health failed Hutchings chose to come to Yosemite, and in 1862 he purchased a hotel that became known as Hutchings House. The hotel was very primitive; only sheets

of muslin hung to separate the rooms. Hutchings built a sawmill along Yosemite Creek to prepare the lumber for more effective partitions and for a time employed John Muir to run the mill.

When the Yosemite Grant was set aside in 1864, Hutchings became embroiled in lengthy and bitter litigation with the government as a property owner dispossessed. His political fortunes changed, however, in 1880, when he was named to succeed Galen Clark as Yosemite guardian. He worked in that capacity for four years.

Hutchings' many writings outlived him. His *Hutchings' Illustrated California Magazine* is full of historical gems, and he published a series of guidebooks to the Yosemite Valley and the Big Trees. His most famous work is *In the Heart of the Sierras,* which is representative of the best travel writing of that era.

Killed in a wagon accident on the Old Big Oak Flat Road in Yosemite Valley in 1902, Hutchings is buried in the Yosemite Cemetery.

John Muir

For his efforts on behalf of the park, John Muir has come to be recognized as the most significant individual in the history of Yosemite. This reputation is certainly deserved; Muir's contributions to the place through the years were considerable, particularly his efforts to create Yosemite National Park in 1890. He will also long be associated with the park thanks to his eloquent, loving writings.

John Muir first visited Yosemite in 1868 and returned the following summer to work as a shepherd in the high country. Late in 1869, he could no longer resist the lure of Yosemite Valley and found work doing odd jobs there for James Mason Hutchings. He built a small cabin on Yosemite Creek and began a long-term residence in his beloved Yosemite.

Muir roamed and studied the park, learning its aspects as intimately as he could. He became renowned as a guide and entertained Asa Gray, William Keith, Ralph Waldo Emerson, and other luminaries of the day. His marathon hikes with few or no provisions have become legendary. He recorded his experiences and documented the natural world around him in a series of journals.

In 1871 Muir published a newspaper article about Yosemite; it was the first of a series of articles and books he would write during his life. Topics of his writing included the glaciers, the forests, winter storms, and everything else about Yosemite that came to fascinate him.

In the mid-1870s Muir married and left Yosemite, beginning a new life in Martinez, California. In 1889 he returned to the park with Robert Underwood Johnson. It was during this visit that the two hatched a campaign to establish Yosemite National Park. Using articles, personal visits, and other lobbying efforts, the two saw the 1890 act to create the national park through to its successful passage.

Muir was later to write *My First Summer in the Sierra* and *The Yosemite,* both of which—among many others—would become Yosemite classics. His tireless work in opposition to the damming of the park's Hetch Hetchy Valley (a fight that he lost) drained him physically and contributed to his death in 1914.

David and Jennie Curry

The Curry name is synonymous with the concession operation in Yosemite, and these lively people were pioneer innkeepers in the park. In 1899 they moved to California from Indiana and established a small camp in the eastern end of Yosemite Valley. Starting with seven tents for guests and a dining tent that seated twenty, the Currys initiated an enterprise that experienced immediate growth.

By the end of their first season, the camp had increased to twenty-five tents, and almost three hundred guests had been accommodated. The operation soon became known as Camp Curry, and thanks to their warm hospitality and outgoing personalities the Currys prospered.

David Curry specialized in entertaining his guests with both disarming informality and brash showmanship. Every night at the campfire, people were encouraged to add wood to the fire and, while it burned, to tell stories or lead the group in songs. Curry also revitalized the Firefall, the spectacle that involved pushing burning embers from the brink of Glacier Point to create a stream of fire down the cliff face.

"Mother" Curry, as she was affectionately called, was considerably less flamboyant, but she continued the Camp Curry tradition when David died in 1917. She was assisted by various family members and saw her camp grow to include lodging for thirteen hundred guests.

In 1925 the Curry Camping Company and the Yosemite National Park Company merged to form a single concession operation known as the Yosemite Park & Curry Company that operated until 1993.

Ansel Adams

The man who best communicated the beauty of Yosemite through photography during the twentieth century was Ansel Adams, and his influence continues to be felt. His images have been a source of inspiration, delight, and enjoyment to millions of people, and they have defined the Yosemite landscape for many. Further, he was a dogged conservationist who worked hard to protect the environment he photographed with such skill.

Interestingly, Ansel Adams was a gifted artist in two fields. He almost became a professional pianist, but the camera won out, particularly as Adams became more and more attached to Yosemite. After moving to the valley in 1920 to run the Sierra Club Lodge, he made the acquaintance of the proprietor of Best's Studio, painter Harry Best, who allowed Ansel the use of a piano. It brought Adams in contact with Best's daughter Virginia, whom he later married.

For several years Adams worked as a commercial photographer doing publicity pictures for the Curry Company and other such jobs. As the years passed, his promotional work gave way increasingly to his more artistic expression. His prints were offered for sale in gift shops and at Best's Studio, and before long he was gaining national recognition for his fine landscape work.

Many of his photographs were used to illustrate the beauty of natural areas that environmental groups hoped to have protected by Congress, and he undertook special assignments from the National Park Service to photograph the national parks. His landscapes became well known for their detail, tonal ranges, unique composition, and fine printing. A multitude of awards were bestowed upon Adams for his photographic excellence.

He remained active as a photographer and conservationist until his death in 1984, teaching, lecturing, lobbying, and making new images all the while. Best's Studio is now operated as the Ansel Adams Gallery, and a peak on Yosemite's eastern boundary was named for him in 1985.

Selected Yosemite Place Names

Ahwahnee

The local Native American name for both a large village near Yosemite Falls and for the greater Yosemite Valley. The people were known as the Ahwahneechees. Lafayette Bunnell reported that the name meant "deep, grassy valley," although this is unsubstantiated. Linguists believe that "place of a gaping mouth" is the correct translation.

Big Oak Flat

A small town near Yosemite's northwestern boundary from which the Highway 120 route took its original name. The massive oak (reportedly ten feet in diameter) that inspired the name is long since dead, the victim of miners' axes in the 1860s.

Chilnualna

This name, common in the Wawona area, is of unknown origin and meaning. An unsupported theory suggests its meaning is "leaping water."

Clark

Yosemite Valley's first guardian, appointed in 1864, and the first non-native to find the Mariposa Grove of Big Trees was Galen Clark. His name now graces a mountain, a mountain range, and a viewpoint on the way to Nevada Fall.

Conness

A senator from California in the 1860s, John Conness introduced the bill in Congress that set aside Yosemite Valley and the Mariposa Grove of Big Trees as a state preserve. Mount Conness is an imposing peak on the park boundary north of Tioga Pass.

Crane Flat

Most probably named for a group of sandhill cranes encountered there by Lafayette Bunnell (John Muir also noted cranes at the location), although some assert the origin was a man named Crean who at one time resided at the spot.

Curry

David and Jennie "Mother" Curry established a small tent camp for the public in Yosemite Valley in 1899. It grew to become Camp Curry and later Curry Village. The merger of their operation with the Yosemite Park Company resulted in the Yosemite Park & Curry Company, a longtime concessioner.

Dana

Josiah Whitney's California Geological Survey named a prominent peak east of Tuolumne Meadows for James Dwight Dana in 1863. Dana was a Yale professor and considered the foremost American geologist of his time.

El Capitan

This massive granite cliff was named by the Mariposa Battalion in 1851. "El Capitan" is the Spanish equivalent of the local Native American name, "Too-tok-ah-noo-lah." Other names assigned the rock at one time or another were Crane Mountain and Giant's Tower (go Giants!).

El Portal

This is Spanish for "gateway" or "entrance" and was used to name the terminus of the Yosemite Valley Railroad on the park's western doorstep. Now a small town on Highway 140, the site is slated to house the park's headquarters. Because of its searing summer heat, some have dubbed the place "Hell Portal."

Glen Aulin

James McCormick, at the behest of R. B. Marshall of the USGS, named this idyllic spot on the Tuolumne River with the Gaelic phrase for "beautiful valley" or glen in the early 1900s. A High Sierra camp was built there in 1927.

Half Dome

Credit the Mariposa Battalion with describing this split mountain as a half-dome. Of all the landmarks in Yosemite, Half Dome has worn the most names over the years, among them Rock of Ages, North Dome, South Dome, Sentinel Dome, Tis-sa-ack, Cleft Rock, Goddess of Liberty, Mt. Abraham Lincoln, and Spirit of the Valley. Somehow a t-shirt imprinted with the phrase "I climbed the Goddess of Liberty" wouldn't quite work.

Happy Isles

One of Yosemite Valley's early guardians named the three small islets on the Merced River for the emotion he enjoyed while exploring them ("no one can visit them without for the while forgetting the grinding strife of his world and being happy"). For years this was the site of a fish hatchery.

Hetch Hetchy

Hetch Hetchy bears a Native American name that has been interpreted in several ways. The most popular is that it means a kind of grass or plant with edible seeds that abounded in the valley. Some believe Hetchy means "tree" and Hetch Hetchy refers to two yellow pine trees that grew at the entrance to the place. At one time a remarkably beautiful companion valley to Yosemite Valley, the Hetch Hetchy Valley was dammed by the damned city of San Francisco in the 1920s.

Illilouette

This French-sounding name is actually an English transliteration (poor indeed!) of the Native American word "Too-lool-a-we-ack." James Mason Hutchings opined that it means "the place beyond which was the great rendezvous of the Yosemite Indians for hunting deer."

Lembert Dome

Lembert

John Baptiste Lembert was an early settler in the Tuolumne Meadows region. He built a cabin at the soda springs in Tuolumne, and his name is attached to the granite dome nearby.

Lyell

Yosemite's highest peak (13,114 feet) was named for Sir Charles Lyell, an eminent English geologist, by the California Geological Survey in 1863.

Mariposa

The Spanish word for "butterfly" was first applied to a land grant, later to the community, and then to the county. Because Mariposa County encompassed the south end of Yosemite when Galen Clark discovered them in 1857, the sequoias there were named the Mariposa Grove of Big Trees.

Merced

The Moraga party named this river, which originates in Yosemite's high country, when they crossed it in the San Joaquin Valley. This was in 1806, five days after the feast day of Our Lady of Mercy, which is why the river was formally known as El Rio de Nuestra Señora de la Merced (River of Our Lady of Mercy). All other names utilizing "Merced" in Yosemite are derived from the river's name.

Mono

At what is now known as Mono Lake, the resident Native Americans harvested, ate, and traded millions of alkali fly pupae—a favorite foodstuff of the native people of the region. The Shoshonean tribe grew to be known as the Mona or Mono, a name derived from the Yokuts word "monoi" or "monai," meaning "flies." Many landmarks east of Yosemite bear this name.

Nevada

The Mariposa Battalion assigned this name to the waterfall on the Merced River in 1851. The word signifies "snow" in Spanish, and members of the battalion felt this was appropriate because the fall was in the Sierra Nevada and because the white, foaming water was reminiscent of a vast avalanche.

Olmsted

A turnout from Tioga Road near Tenaya Lake with a remarkable view was named for Frederick Law Olmsted Sr. and Jr. The senior Olmsted was involved in the creation of the 1864 Yosemite Grant and served as chairman of the first board of Yosemite Valley commissioners. His son worked as an NPS planner in Yosemite and had a position on the Yosemite Advisory Board.

Sierra Nevada

This is the Spanish phrase for "snowy mountain range." Father Pedro Font applied it to California's greatest range of mountains when he glimpsed it from near Antioch in 1776. Because "sierra" implies plural mountains, it is both grammatically and politically incorrect to use the term "Sierras." If you do you will be castigated by self-righteous Yosemite word snobs.

Stoneman

A large hotel built by the State of California in 1885 once stood in the meadow just north of Curry Village. Known as the Stoneman House for then-Governor George Stoneman, it burned in 1896. The meadow and nearby bridge still bear the name.

Tenaya

The chief of the resident tribe when the Mariposa Battalion entered Yosemite Valley in 1851 was named Tenaya. The battalion first encountered the Native Americans living near the banks of a lake near Tuolumne Meadows that they called Tenaya Lake.

Tioga

This in an Iroquois word meaning "where it forks," "swift current," or "gate." Miners at work on the Sierra crest near Yosemite established the Tioga Mining District in 1878, apparently importing the name from Pennsylvania or New York.

Tuolumne

A tribe residing in the Sierra foothills near Knights Ferry was known as "Taulamne," reportedly pronounced Tu-ah-lum'-ne. This name was applied to the river originating in Yosemite that flowed through their territory.

Vogelsang

Colonel Benson, an Army officer and acting superintendent of Yosemite National Park from 1905 to 1908, named a peak south of Tuolumne Meadows for either Alexander Vogelsang or his brother Charles, both of whom were affiliated with California Fish and Game. The German word "vogelsang" refers to birdsong, which is apt for the site of the Vogelsang High Sierra Camp.

Wawona

Popular opinion has it that "wawona" is a Native American word for "big tree": the sequoias were considered sacred and called "woh-woh'-nah." The word is formed in imitation of the hooting of an owl, which bird is said to have been sacred to the native people, the guardian spirit and deity of the sequoias.

White Wolf

A meadow on the old route of the Tioga Road was named by John Meyer, who, while pursuing Native Americans, came to a temporary camp of the band's chief. His name was White Wolf.

Yosemite

This name was assigned to the world's most beautiful valley by the Mariposa Battalion in 1851. The exact meaning of the name is disputed. Lafayette Bunnell, a member of the battalion, later wrote that it signified "grizzly bear" (derived from the Miwok word for the bears, "uzumati"). Others consider it a corruption of the Miwok word "Yo-che-ma-te," which means "some among them are killers" and is said to have referred to the Ahwahneechee people of Yosemite.

Tuolumne Meadows from Tioga Road

Great gray owl

3 | Yosemite's Natural World

Yosemite is filled with living things of every description existing in a remarkable setting created by the various forces of nature. From its famous black bears and big trees to nocturnal owls, seldom-seen reptiles, pesky mosquitoes, and mysterious fungi, the park is abundant with flora and fauna that are rich and varied. Because wildlife is protected in Yosemite, the park has served as an "island" sanctuary of sorts, where natural processes have continued and biological diversity is still great. Other factors contributing to this favorable situation for animals and plants are the great range of elevations within the park (from 2,000 to 13,000 feet) and the corresponding variety of living conditions that change with the elevation. Though inanimate, other natural objects and processes contribute to the ever-evolving Yosemite scene. Geological workings are constant, waterfalls ebb and flow, and meteorological forces add variety and life to the landscape. And because the setting has been so unchanged and undeveloped, Yosemite National Park is even more significant as a mountain laboratory of the natural world.

There are differing views as to the processes that shaped Yosemite, and most descriptions of Yosemite geology are rife with technical jargon, geological gobble-dygook, and scientific names. This is an attempt to make the processes that created Yosemite's landscape of granite and water more understandable for the layperson. And with it comes the promise that words like batholith, pyroclastic, and subduction will not be used.

cooled and hardened before making it to the surface, great areas of granite rock.

This process occurred in a series of pulses over a period of some 150 million years. When it was complete, a mountain range had been formed that ran in a rough line parallel to the west coast. Although it was largely covered by the continental crust (primarily sedimentary rock), this ancestral Sierra Nevada range was probably similar

Look for "erratic" boulders on Yosemite's peaks and ridges. These large rocks at Olmsted Point were transported from distant sources by glacial ice.

Once upon a time, about 500 million years ago, sediment was deposited in layers on the ocean floor at the west edge of what would later become the continent of North America. This sediment was consolidated into rocks such as sandstone, chert, shale, and limestone. Neither the landmass of the developing continent nor the landmass covered by sedimentary rock under the ocean was stationary, however.

Time passed (about 300 million years or so) and the two landmasses moved towards each other and met, and then some exciting geology took place. The rock beneath the ocean was forced under the continental landmass with interesting results. The process caused the rock of the ocean plate to become very hot and liquefy into magma (which is the molten rock that shoots out of volcanoes). This hot liquid rose up under the edge of the continent to form volcanoes and, where it

to the present Cascade Range of volcanoes. In some places the mountains may have been as high as 13,000 feet.

For approximately the next 55 million years, the main force at work in the ancestral Sierra was erosion (we all know what that is, right?). The volcanoes were worn away by wind and water, as was the continental crust that sat on top of the great granite mass created by the molten rock described above. The rock that eroded away was carried by rivers and streams into California's Central Valley. When this period of erosion was complete, what was to become the Sierra Nevada—now primarily exposed granite—stood only a few thousand feet high.

Everything was going along fine with the developing Sierra until, one day about 25 million years ago, the landmasses meeting along the present-day San Andreas Fault began to move again. The result was that the block upon which the Sierra sat was uplifted at its eastern edge and tilted towards the west. It is estimated that the tilt raised peaks on Yosemite's eastern edge as much as 11,000 feet.

Following uplift and tilt, river courses in the Yosemite region became steeper, and the erosive effect of their waters increased. The Merced River, for example, began to carve the granite much more sharply, and Yosemite Valley was deepened as a canyon. The Sierra Nevada began to show much greater surface relief and started to take on the form we know today.

About two or three million years ago, the earth's climate began to cool. Because of its extreme height, glaciers and ice fields covered the crest of the Sierra Nevada. At its most extensive, the ice covered over half of Yosemite and sent glaciers down many of the valleys that had been created by erosion.

Glaciers tore loose large quantities of rock as they moved, carving U-shaped canyons and valleys, polishing rock faces, and breaking spires, domes, and various other rock formations along fractures, or joints. The glaciers carried the broken rock as rubble and deposited it along the edges of their paths.

This glacial period consisted of an unknown number of glaciations—perhaps as many as ten. The last glaciation reached its maximum between 20,000 and 15,000 years ago. At that point, the earth's climate began to warm again, glaciers receded, and nonglacial erosion became the main geological force working in Yosemite once more.

Yosemite Valley is one location in the park whose appearance has changed considerably since glacial times. Because glaciers dumped enormous quantities of rock and rubble at its western end, the valley's outflow was stopped and water covered its floor. Geologists call this ancient body of water Lake Yosemite. Over a period of ten thousand years, sediment and silt washed down from the park's higher regions and filled the lake, creating the flat, dry valley floor we know today.

Yosemite's landscape continues to change even now. While the geological processes are not dramatic (some changes take millions of years), erosion continues, avalanches occur, and rockslides are common. The geologic story goes on in Yosemite and provides us with a better understanding of the extraordinary scenery that has made the park famous.

Glaciers carved the U-shaped Yosemite Valley

Nineteenth-century scientists were as puzzled by Yosemite Valley's origin as many first-time visitors are today. Their efforts to explain what they saw resulted in a variety of theories about the creation of the valley's sheer walls and spectacular waterfalls.

Josiah D. Whitney, California's state geologist and director of the California Geological Survey, made many of the first studies of Yosemite during the 1860s. In his view, Yosemite Valley had not been formed by erosion or glaciation or any other traditional geologic force. He believed that a valley so deep could only have been created by a collapse of the section of the earth below it. Because Whitney was an accomplished Harvard professor with quite a reputation as a scholar and scientist, his theory gained some acceptance.

At about the same time, mountain wanderer John Muir (see page 51) was making observations of his own. He, too, was fascinated with the geologic history of Yosemite Valley. Muir advanced the hypothesis that it was the action of glaciers, an "over-sweeping ice current," that had carved the Yosemite landscape. He worked to popularize the theory and it came to be known as "Muir's discovery."

View of Half Dome from Olmsted Point

Whitney was not impressed nor convinced. He characterized Muir's ideas as absurd and passed them off as the ravings of a "mere shepherd." Doggedly, Whitney defended his "cataclysm" theory for some twenty years, until his death.

While Muir was not correct in all the details of the work of the glaciers, he was remarkably close. Later studies proved the basic soundness of his theory and helped establish John Muir's reputation as a thoughtful and insightful student of the Sierra.

Joints Shaped the Rocks

The variety of rock shapes and formations that occur in Yosemite is impressive. From blocks to domes to spires to arches to sheets, there is tremendous diversity in the granitic terrain. How did these structures come to be?

All of Yosemite's unusual landmarks (with but a few exceptions) resulted from the existence of fractures within their original rock structures. These fractures, called joints, are the lines upon which the rock has been broken. They create zones of weakness within the granite that yield to the action of glaciers and to the intrusion of water.

Joints occur both vertically and horizontally, and some are inclined (for example, the Three Brothers formation was created along inclined joints). Vertical jointing is most prevalent and produced features like the face of Half Dome and the Cathedral Spires. Where vertical and horizontal joints intersect, the result is rectangular blocks.

Half Dome and El Capitan are representative of very sparse jointing. Their resistance to erosion and glaciation has kept them practically unchanged for thousands of years. Incidentally, there probably was no other half of Half Dome. Geologists believe that only 20 percent of the dome's original size has been lost.

The type of jointing most dramatic in the evolution of Yosemite landforms is sheeting, which results in the concentric joints that lead to the creation of domes. As overlying rock falls away, pressure is relieved on the granite. It expands upward and fractures result. The concentric fractures break off like the different layers of an onion in a process called exfoliation.

Yosemite Waterfalls

The collection of waterfalls in Yosemite National Park is unequaled anywhere in the world. And nowhere else have so many spectacular waterfalls been concentrated in so small an area as Yosemite Valley. What's most remarkable is the number of park waterfalls that are free-leaping; they make their descent without being broken on intervening ledges or outcroppings. The park's glacial geology is responsible for this unique situation.

While the glaciers carved major watercourses like Yosemite Valley very deeply, lateral tributary ice streams cut much more slowly and less effectively. The result was "hanging valleys," and streams and creeks that previously had fed directly into primary rivers became routed over the brinks of lofty precipices into the more deeply carved canyons below them. Today these waters still leap into space over sheer walls, as Yosemite's waterfalls. Bridalveil Fall is a great example of a waterfall originating from a hanging valley.

Other waterfalls were created as the glaciers moved along and dislocated large blocks of granite from streambeds. The rock gave way along joints and took on shapes like steps in a staircase. This was the process responsible for Vernal and Nevada falls, which drop in two major steps from Little Yosemite Valley. Known as the "Giant Staircase," this landform is well viewed from Glacier Point.

Yosemite's waterfalls are at peak flow during the months of April, May, and June, when 75 percent of the annual snowmelt occurs. May is usually the best single month for waterfall watching. By July most of the surface runoff is gone, and

Upper and Lower Yosemite Falls from Glacier Point

many falls either dry up or are reduced to a trickle. Some falls (Bridalveil, for example) rarely dry up because the soil of their watersheds holds more water longer.

Not all the waterfalls in the park are large, spectacular, or permanent. Many cascades exist where streambeds were resistant to the glaciers but some gouging and polishing did occur. In those cases channels steepened, and now water spills over irregularly fractured granite or down gradual

The Spirits of Yosemite Falls—A Native American Legend

In the waters just below Cho'lok (Yosemite Falls) live the Po'loti, a group of dangerous spirit women. In the old days there was a village a short distance from the falls. A maiden from this village went to the stream for a basket of water. She dipped the basket into the stream as usual but brought it up full of snakes. She went farther upstream and tried again, but with the same result. She tried repeatedly, each time a little farther upstream, but always drew a basketful of snakes. Finally, she reached the pool at the foot of Cho'lok, and a sudden, violent wind blew her into it. During the night she gave birth to a child that she wrapped in a blanket and took home the next morning. The girl's mother was very curious and soon took the blanket off the baby in order to see it. Immediately a violent gale arose and blew the entire village and its inhabitants into the same pool. Nothing has ever been seen or heard of them since.

—from *Legends of the Yosemite Miwok*, compiled by Frank LaPena, Craig D. Bates, and Steven P. Medley (El Portal: Yosemite Association, 1993).

cliff faces. Other falls are ephemeral: they appear only during heavy thunderstorms or at the peak of the spring runoff. As abruptly as the rain ends, so do these fleeting displays.

In winter, park waterfalls have a different beauty. Because the snowpack prevents soil moisture from freezing, water continues to flow in the falls. But they become edged with ice, and droplets of water actually freeze as they descend through space. When this freezing occurs in a large volume, "frazil ice" is the result. Streams at the base of the waterfalls become filled with ice crystals that create ice slush. As it moves, the frazil ice adheres to any object below freezing and can clog streambeds.

The most famous winter waterfall phenomenon is the ice cone that builds up at the base of Upper Yosemite Fall. Ice slabs that have frozen at the fall's edges fall and gently freezing spray collects, and the ice cone grows, sometimes to a height of three hundred feet, covering some four acres. The cone usually melts away by April.

Waterfalls of Yosemite Valley

Yosemite Falls	2,425 feet	North wall, eastern end
Sentinel Falls	2,000 feet	South wall, west of Sentinel Rock
Ribbon Fall	1,612 feet	North wall, west of El Capitan
Staircase Falls	1,300 feet	South wall, behind Curry Village
Royal Arch Cascade	1,250 feet	North wall, west of Washington Column
Silver Strand Falls	1,170 feet	South wall, far west end
Horsetail Fall	1,000 feet	North wall, east side of El Capitan
Lehamite Falls	uncertain	North wall, in Indian Canyon
Bridalveil Fall	620 feet	South wall, west end
The Cascades	uncertain	North wall, 2 miles west of Yosemite Valley
Nevada Fall	594 feet	Easternmost end of Merced River Canyon
Illilouette Fall	370 feet	Panorama Cliffs southeast of Glacier Point

The Twelve Highest Waterfalls in the World

Angel Falls	3,212 feet	Venezuela
Tugela Falls	3,110 feet	South Africa
Utigordsfossen	2,625 feet	Norway
Mongefossen	2,540 feet	Norway
Gocta Cataracts	2,532 feet	Peru
Mutarazi	2,499 feet	Zimbabwe
Yosemite Falls	2,425 feet	Yosemite
Espelandsfoss	2,307 feet	Norway
Ostre Mardalsfoss	2,151 feet	Norway
Tyssestrengene	2,123 feet	Norway
Sentinel Falls	2,000 feet	Yosemite
Cuquenan Falls	2,000 feet	Venezuela

Natural Events

Fires

Fire has long played a role in Yosemite's natural world. It is a major ecological force, with impacts similar to those of other natural phenomena such as floods, earthquakes, and hurricanes. Wildland fires, defined as all fires that burn in natural environments, greatly influence park ecosystems. Prior to the appearance of humans here, the ingredients for fire were largely controlled by climate. With the arrival of Native Americans and later Euro-American settlers, sources of fire and fuels were modified as people changed their environment.

Wildland fire fosters new plant growth, expands wildlife populations, and removes dead trees and litter from the forest floor. Also, fires kill shrubs and trees that are invading grasslands. Following fire, healthy regrowth occurs. Accordingly, fire is recognized as an instrument of change and a catalyst for biological diversity and healthy ecosystems.

On occasion, wildfires (unwanted fires in the natural environment) originating in national parks burn forests, towns, or homes with devastating results. Because of these negative impacts, people often mistakenly consider all fires to be destructive forces. However, properly managed fire, referred to as prescribed fire, can be an effective natural resource management tool.

In Yosemite, fires usually are classified as either natural or human-induced. Natural fires are usually started by lightning. Natural fires may be monitored and allowed to burn under prescribed conditions; wildfires are those that humans seek to extinguish. Prescribed fires are initiated by humans under predetermined conditions and are used to manage certain types of landscapes, for reducing fuel buildup around campground areas or providing proper soil conditions for the germination of such species as the giant sequoia. Among the other benefits of prescribed burning are:

- Insect pest control
- Removal of undesirable plants that compete with wanted species
- Addition of nutrients, from ashes that remain after a fire, for trees and other vegetation
- Removal of undergrowth so that sunlight reaches the forest floor, to encourage growth of native species
- Clearing of congested forest areas to prevent the accumulation of fuels

The Fires of 1990

In August 1990, lightning from intense thunderstorms along the west side of Yosemite ignited about forty different fires. Because the fires threatened human life and property, park staff immediately began to suppress them.

Burned trees at Smith Peak

But two of the fires, known as the A-Rock and the Steamboat, quickly grew beyond control. A number of factors contributed to the severity of the fires, among them high winds, drought conditions, large amounts of available fuel, and steep terrain. The fires quickly advanced to become the most intense type, crown fires, which burn through the top layer of foliage on a tree, known as the canopy.

Containment and ultimate control of the two fires took some two weeks, more than three thousand firefighters, and more than $13 million. The A-Rock fire eventually encompassed 18,100 acres, while the Steamboat fire covered about 5,280 acres. Damage was estimated at about $26 million and included the loss of homes (primarily in the park inholding known as Foresta) and the loss of income for concessioner and gateway community businesses.

More than twenty years later, the effects of the fires could still be seen. From the Big Oak Flat Road a few miles above Yosemite Valley, the Foresta region still appeared starkly devoid of mature trees. Vegetation matures slowly, and it will be many more years before some semblance of the area's previous coniferous forest returns. Along stretches of Wawona Road between Yosemite Valley and Chinquapin (the turnoff to Glacier Point) many acres of forest burned, and damage is visible along the roadway where wildfires swept through the area again in 2009, burning some of the same areas.

Floods

Since Yosemite was first occupied by those who recorded their experiences in writing, its natural watercourses have flooded periodically. In 1862, homesteader James Lamon was forced from his home by the rising Merced River, and in 1958 the Wawona Covered Bridge was damaged by the waters of the South Fork.

A flooded meadow in Yosemite Valley

History has shown that flooding by the Merced is not uncommon—rather, it should be expected. Specifically, major floods in Yosemite Valley occurred in 1937, 1950, 1955, and 1964. Such events were the result of various factors, but the most common was warm winter rains falling on accumulated snow up to the highest elevations of the park. When such conditions occur, the existing river channels cannot accommodate the huge quantities of runoff, and water flows into meadows, forests, and developed areas. Because of the relative regularity with which flooding occurs in Yosemite Valley, its floodplain has been carefully mapped.

The Flood of 1997

In the early morning hours of January 1, 1997, rain fell on packed snow in Yosemite at elevations up to 9,500 feet. The deluge from the storm created a high volume of water rarely seen in the rivers and waterfalls of the park.

Runoff peaked in Yosemite Valley at about 11 p.m. on January 2, and streams and rivers overflowed their banks and carved new channels. Over two thousand people (employees and visitors alike) were stranded in the valley when all three access roads were closed. Evacuation finally took place after the water subsided, downed trees were removed, and road repairs were completed.

The effects of the flood were wide-ranging. Water channels were widened, riverbanks were scoured and eroded, and trees and shrubs were uprooted, but the flood's impact on the natural scene was not major. On the other hand, human-made structures and systems were seriously affected. Electrical service was shut down, mud and rockslides blocked roads and damaged power poles, sewer lines broke, and campgrounds, buildings, and roads were flooded. In some cases, large sections of roadway were washed away or underlying roadbeds were destroyed.

While initial repairs and recovery efforts were being made, Yosemite Valley was closed to the public for three months. For the next two and a half years, repairs to the Arch Rock Road and Highway 140 continued, requiring regular road closures; unrestricted access to Yosemite Valley was finally achieved again in October 2000.

1997 Flood Statistics

- More than 1.4 miles of riverbank and 550 acres of meadows were eroded in Yosemite Valley.

- About half of Yosemite Valley's 900 campsites were flooded. Many have since been eliminated and are not likely to be replaced.

- Nine road bridges in the valley suffered damage and required repair. The footbridge at Happy Isles has been removed.

- A 300-foot section of the 14-inch sewer line located beneath Arch Rock Road was destroyed, severing the valley sewer system and contaminating the Merced River.

- Over 350 motel and cabin units at Yosemite Lodge were flooded and removed.

- Over 200 concession employee quarters were flooded, and 439 employees were displaced.

- At least ten archaeological sites sustained heavy damage, and some cultural features and artifacts were completely removed.

- The estimated cost of recovering from the damage and effects of the flood is $178 million.

Yosemite Plant Life

There are over fifteen hundred different types of plants in Yosemite. They range from the grand sequoias to tiny fungi and lichen. What follows is a brief overview of Yosemite flora with information on how to find out much more.

Trees along the Merced River in autumn

Trees

Both cone-bearing and broad-leaved trees appear in abundance within Yosemite National Park. Conifers, the trees that bear cones, do not shed all of their leaves or needles annually, and this has led to their designation as "evergreens." Most of the broad-leaved trees drop their leaves each year.

The Conifers

At least eighteen different species of conifers occur in the park. About half of them are pines. Most common at lower elevations are the ponderosa (or yellow) pine and the Jeffrey pine. The ponderosa, abundant in Yosemite Valley, has yellow-orange bark, needles in groups of three, bark scales that fit together like a jigsaw puzzle, and a trunk up to six feet in diameter. The Jeffrey pine looks much like the ponderosa but grows at higher elevations (Glacier Point is a typical locality). If in doubt, smell the bark. The Jeffrey exudes a sweet odor like vanilla or pineapple.

The two typical high-elevation pines are the lodgepole and the whitebark. The lodgepole has needles in twos, yellowish bark, and small cones. The whitebark features needles in bunches of five and purplish, pitchy cones, and tends to be dwarfed at tree line.

Other notable conifers are the red and white firs. Large forests of these trees can be seen along Tioga and Glacier Point roads. White firs occur between 3,500 and 8,000 feet and have 2-inch needles that twist off the branch and 3- to-5-inch cones. Red firs, in contrast, have shorter needles that curl upwards and larger cones (5 to 8 inches), and grow between 6,000 and 9,000 feet.

Broad-Leaved Trees

Almost without exception, these trees are deciduous: they lose their leaves in the fall. As the leaves die they take on different hues, such as orange, yellow, and brown. It is the foliage of the broad-leaved trees, then, that provides us with Yosemite's sometimes spectacular "fall color." The deciduous trees are less varied than the conifers in the park.

There are several different oak species in Yosemite. In the valley, the California black oak is distinctive. It grows to heights of 75 feet, has dark gray to black bark, and produces large acorns that were a staple of the Native American diet. The other common oak is the canyon live oak, which has holly-like evergreen leaves that it keeps all winter.

Other conspicuous broad-leaved trees are the mountain dogwood, which produces beautiful and delicate whitish green flowers each spring, and the quaking aspen, known for its paper-thin white bark and the rustling of its often-colorful leaves with the slightest breeze.

Along streams and rivers, particularly at lower elevations, one will encounter cottonwoods (leaves are bright green on top and light below), willows (slender pointed leaves), and alders (dark green leaves with obvious veins and small teeth).

Ponderosa pine cones on the forest floor

Flowering Plants

The spectacular geography of Yosemite, with its elevations ranging from 2,000 to over 13,000 feet, supports a wonderful wildflower garden, not to mention shrubs, grasses, sedges, rushes, ferns, and fungi. The differing temperatures, precipitation levels, and growing seasons ensure that a wide assortment of plants find conditions to their liking at locations throughout the park.

The blooming season is a long one in Yosemite. It starts in the foothills in April and May and gradually moves upslope as the weather warms and the snow melts. It doesn't reach the park's highest elevations until August, when flowers make a brief two-month appearance. All told, the wildflower season in Yosemite lasts a full six months!

For the student of botany, Yosemite is indeed a remarkable classroom. Within the park is some of the most distinctive vegetation in the world. Because natural processes have been allowed to continue and because little disruption of the physical environment has occurred, plant life is varied and rich.

Alpine lily

Western azalea

Sneezeweed

Fleabane daisy

Wandering daisy

Lewis's monkeyflower

Mariposa lily

Western monkshood

Pussypaws

Scarlet gilia

Snow plant

Sierra stickseed

The Giant Sequoias

After its granite cliffs and domes and its spectacular waterfalls, Yosemite is best known for its famous big trees, the giant sequoias (*Sequoiadendron giganteum*). In fact, the 1864 Yosemite Grant set aside as a protected park only Yosemite Valley and the Mariposa Grove of Big Trees. These towering monarchs were recognized for their special qualities early in history, and they continue to inspire awe to this day.

The mature big trees can be recognized by their huge, columnar trunks that are free of branches for 100 to 150 feet above the ground. The foliage is blue-green and individual leaves create rounded sprays, unlike the flattened branchlets of the incense cedar. The bark is quite fibrous, can be 4 to 24 inches thick, and is cinnamon brown in color. This bark covering is nonresinous and very fire-resistant. Sequoia wood is pink when cut, then darkens to red. It is amazingly resistant to decay (many downed trees remain intact on the ground for years). Cones are quite small (2 or 3 inches), are abundant, and produce several hundred seeds each.

The giant sequoias grow from these tiny seeds that are no larger than flakes of oatmeal. You would have to amass over 90,000 seeds to produce a pound of them. Upon germination, a one-inch seedling results, and these seedlings grow into young trees through the years. These youngsters are characterized by a fairly symmetrical, cone-shaped appearance with a sharply pointed crown.

At seven or eight hundred years of age, sequoias are mature, have just about reached their maximum height, and have developed a rounded top. Some mature trees that have been burned are noted for their "snag tops." When fire damages the bases of the trees, water supply to their upper reaches is limited and the tops of the trees die. The trees remain healthy, but their appearance suggests the hazards they have survived and the effects of age.

Scientists believe that the giant sequoia is the largest living thing in the world (though this is sometimes disputed). The trees stop growing upward at about eight hundred years of age, but they continue to add bulk. Maximum height seems to be about 320 feet, and diameters vary depending on where the measurements are taken (there is quite a swelling at the base of each sequoia). Some trees at the base are over 35 feet in diameter, while at about twenty feet above the ground, that size drops to about 20 feet.

It is hard to grasp the immensity of the sequoias. One example that provides perspective is the largest branch on the Grizzly Giant tree in the Mariposa Grove. It is over six feet in diameter. At that size it is larger than the trunks of the largest specimens of most trees east of the Mississippi River. It is also larger than many of the conifers in Yosemite.

Despite their longevity, giant sequoias are not the oldest living things. That distinction is reserved for the bristlecone pines, which may live to be 5,000 years old. Sequoias are known to live at least 3,200 years, and John Muir reported finding an individual 4,000 years old.

Giant sequoia

Giant sequoias occur naturally only in the Sierra Nevada, primarily at elevations between 5,000 and 7,000 feet. In Yosemite there are three groves: the Mariposa Grove (see page 113), the Tuolumne Grove, and the Merced Grove (page 126). Any visit to Yosemite should include a trip to see these impressive trees.

It is important to note that while the two species are related, sequoias are different from redwoods (*Sequoia sempervirens*). Redwoods live on the misty northern California coast and are relatively common there. They are the tallest trees in the world at almost 400 feet, but sequoias are heavier.

Over seventy-five species of mammals have been recorded in Yosemite National Park. What follows are brief descriptions of some of those mammals, particularly those that visitors are likely to see in the course of their stay in the park. As you travel through Yosemite by car, be especially careful to follow the speed limits. Each year several hundred animals are killed by motorists.

Black bear

Black Bear

Many people react to the black bear with both fascination and fear. Because of the multitude of stories that are told about bears throughout the national park system, there are plenty of misconceptions that exist about these largest of park mammals.

Yosemite's black bear is often confused with the grizzly bear, a species that no longer exists in the park. The grizzly once roamed the Sierra Nevada but was eliminated by hunters around the turn of the century. The last grizzly killing in Yosemite occurred in 1895, and the last authentic record of the killing of a grizzly in California is from 1922.

Grizzly bears are considerably more dangerous to humans than are black bears. Occasional black bear incidents do occur, but those mainly result from improper food storage. Never feed the bears, and observe them at a distance (particularly when cubs are present)!

Despite their name, black bears can be brown, blonde, cinnamon, or black. There are no members of the brown bear species (or any other) in Yosemite. Individuals range in size from 250 to 400 pounds, although even bigger bears have been recorded.

Black bears can be observed throughout the park, particularly in the evenings. Many bears enter dens in winter for a period of sleep. Young are born in late winter and leave the den in spring to forage with their mothers.

Black Bears and Human Food

Black bears are omnivores—they will eat practically anything. Typical fare is insects, small rodents, berries, acorns, and seeds. But human food, from hot dogs to cookies, also appeals to park bears; driven by their excellent sense of smell and enormous appetite, they are drawn to it. Once they have had a taste of it, they continue to seek it out from any possible source, including backpacks, picnic tables, ice chests, and cars. Their natural fear of humans fades, and some bears may become aggressive.

Aggressive bears often have to be killed. Each year black bears are killed in Yosemite as a direct result of human carelessness and improper food storage. In 2010, there were nearly five hundred incidents involving bears, resulting in over $100,000 in damage; several bears had to be killed. No bear has ever killed a person in Yosemite National Park. The only way to prevent the continuing loss of bears is to make sure that all food and trash are stored properly.

"Food" includes any item with a scent, regardless of packaging. This includes canned goods, bottles, drinks, and items that you might not consider food, such as soaps, cosmetics, toiletries, perfumes, trash, empty ice chests, and unwashed food-preparation items.

What If You See a Bear?

Never approach a bear, regardless of its size. If you encounter a bear in a developed area of the park or on a hiking trail, act immediately: yell as loudly as possible or, if necessary, throw small stones or sticks toward the bear from a safe distance with the goal of scaring the bear (you don't want to injure it). If others are with you, stand together to present a more intimidating figure, but do not make the bear feel surrounded—you want the bear to run away!

Use caution if you see cubs, as a mother may act aggressively to defend them. Never try to retrieve anything once a bear has it. If you follow these recommendations and act immediately, you should be successful in scaring bears away. Report all bear encounters to a park ranger as soon as possible.

Yosemite Wild Bear Project

A special group of "Keep Bears Wild" products, including t-shirts, enamel pins, and stuffed animal toys, have been developed for sale in Yosemite. Proceeds from the sales of these items directly benefit park bears through the Yosemite Wild Bear Project, a joint effort of the Yosemite Conservancy, DNC Parks and Resorts at Yosemite, and the National Park Service. One of the many programs supported by the project is making bear canisters available for backpackers to rent. Donations are welcome to support the Yosemite Wild Bear Project (call 800-469-7275), and products can be purchased online at yosemiteconservancy.org.

Mule Deer

Having experienced a life free of threat from humans, the mule deer in Yosemite seem almost tame. You are likely to spot one or more of these graceful creatures anywhere in the park, but they are especially obvious in Yosemite Valley and in the Wawona Meadow area.

Despite the fact that they seem unconcerned by humans, mule deer should be treated like any other wild animal. These deer should be given a wide berth and not be fed (nor should any other park animal); many injuries have been caused to

Mule deer

visitors who have disturbed these animals in the course of offering them human food. Even deaths have resulted from gorings and from the blows delivered by the surprisingly sharp hooves of the mule deer. In fact, deer inflict more injuries in Yosemite each year than black bears or any other park animal.

The mule deer takes its name from its large, mulelike ears. Weighing up to two hundred pounds, it is primarily a browsing animal, eating leaves and tender twigs from trees, grass, and other herbs. The male mule deer (the buck) grows antlers each year for use in the mating season, or "rut," each fall. Despite popular belief, the age of a given buck cannot be determined by counting the number of antler points he sports.

Mule deer are very common in Yosemite, chiefly between 3,500 and 8,500 feet. They

---

Bear-Aware Food Storage

Parking areas	Place food in food storage lockers if available, or in your hotel room or cabin (but not your tent cabin). Food must not be stored in vehicles after dark, even in trunks. Don't forget to clear vehicles of food wrappers, crumbs, and baby wipes. Food may be stored out of sight in vehicles with windows closed during daylight hours only, but bear lockers or trailhead bear boxes are still preferable.
Campgrounds	All food must be stored in food storage lockers without exception, day and night. Each campsite contains a food storage locker (bear box) measuring 33" x 45" x 18".
Tent cabins	All food must be stored in food storage lockers, day and night. Never leave items with an odor in your tent.
Hotel rooms and cabins	All food must be kept inside your room or cabin. If you are not in your room, the windows and doors must be closed.
Picnic areas and on the trail	Do not leave food unattended; keep it within arm's reach at all times.
Backpacking	Bear-resistant food canisters are required for overnight hikers. (see page 19).

stay below the snow line in winter, often dropping into the foothills that border the west side of the park. Common predators of the mule deer are the mountain lion and the coyote.

Pika

American Pika

You need to be lucky and adventurous to see a pika in Yosemite. These shy little animals live far from people, in rocky slopes high up near the Sierra crest, along the eastern boundary of the park. Even if you make it up there, you'll need to keep a sharp eye out—pikas are only a few inches long and have gray fur that blends into their rocky home. You are more likely to hear one than see it. If you hear a squeak and cannot identify the animal that made it (marmots and ground squirrels squeak too, but you should be able to see them without too much trouble), look carefully among the rock piles. Pikas look a lot like voles or mice but are actually small rabbits with short ears. Good luck.

If you do find a pika you are seeing one of the most remarkably adapted and scientifically important animals in the Sierra Nevada. Despite living in some of the coldest, windiest parts of the range, they do not hibernate. They stay awake and alive through the winter by making hay, just as farmers do for their livestock. In the summer months, pikas cut pieces of grass and sedge from the area around their dens and leave them on rocks to dry in the sun. Once the hay is ready, they store it in a larder that sustains them all winter. Any pika you do see is probably making hay while the sun shines. If you sit still long enough, you may see one busily scampering back and forth between its plants and its den.

At present, the easiest place (relatively speaking) to see a pika is along the path up Mt. Dana, south of Tioga Pass.

Mountain Lion

Terror-inducing stories abound about these large members of the cat family, but although they are present in Yosemite, they are almost never seen and rarely interact with humans. Also known as cougars, panthers, or pumas, mountain lions prey on other mammals, primarily deer. They are wary of people and go out of their way to avoid contact with park visitors; they are not normally a serious threat to human safety.

Besides deer, the mountain lion also will eat a number of small mammals, including marmots, rabbits, foxes, coyotes, and raccoons, and even porcupines and skunks when the pickings are slim. Because they help to keep Yosemite's deer population in check, mountain lions are considered an important component of the park ecosystem.

Tricks for Observing Animals

Try strolling down a forest trail, or walk along the edge of a meadow. Avoid groups of people, as most animals are easily frightened. Consider the color of your clothing and don't wear white—it makes you too conspicuous. Darker shades are better. Walk slowly. When you see an animal, don't make quick movements. If you should come upon one, such as a deer or a squirrel, continue slowly so as not to alarm it. Stop to watch it when you are still some distance away. If you want to see an animal that has disappeared into a burrow—a marmot, ground squirrel, or mouse—find a comfortable place to sit and remain quiet. Usually it will reappear in a short time to see where you are and what you are doing. Watch for evidence of mammal activities, such as dens, trails in the grass, or kitchen middens where squirrels have cut away and piled the scales of pine cones. Watch, too, for holes dug where pine nuts or acorns have been buried.

—from *Discovering Sierra Mammals* by Russell Grater (El Portal: Yosemite Association, 1997)

Mountain lions can weigh from 75 to 275 pounds. They are 6 to 9 feet long including the tail. They are recognized by their size, solid tan color, and extended tail. Females give birth to a litter of one to six cubs in midsummer every other year. Mountain lions produce a number of catlike sounds, including hisses, growls, and yowls, and their mating call has been likened to the screams of a woman.

Humans and Mountain Lions

While mountain lion attacks on humans are extremely rare, they are possible. Generally, mountain lions are calm, quiet, and elusive. If you spot one, consider yourself privileged! The National Park Service offers the following safety recommendations:

- Do not leave pets or pet food outside and unattended, especially at dawn and dusk. Pets can attract mountain lions into developed areas.

- Avoid hiking alone. Watch children closely and never let them run ahead of you on the trail. Talk to children about mountain lions, and teach them what to do if they meet one (see below).

- Store food according to park regulations.

What If You See a Mountain Lion?

- Never approach a mountain lion, especially if it is feeding or with kittens. Most mountain lions will try to avoid a confrontation. Always give them a way to escape.

- Don't run. Stay calm. Hold your ground, or back away slowly. Face the lion and stand upright. Raise your arms and do all you can to appear larger. If you have small children with you, pick them up.

- If the lion behaves aggressively, wave your arms, shout, and throw objects at it. The goal is to convince it that you are not prey and may be dangerous. If attacked, fight back!

Mountain lion

Coyote

Coyote

Normally a very shy mammal, the Yosemite coyote has become accustomed to the human presence and is commonly seen here, particularly in Yosemite Valley. In winter these doglike creatures often can be viewed hunting in snow-covered meadows.

The coyote is one mammal that makes its presence known by its call. There is nothing more haunting (some would contend frightening) than the late-night howling and barking of a group of coyotes.

Weighing 25 to 30 pounds, coyotes live on small animals (primarily rodents), although fawns and an occasional adult mule deer are taken. Coyotes can be identified by their long, grayish fur (which is lighter on the underside) and a darkish tail.

There are no wolves in Yosemite. If you meet someone who swears that they have seen a wolf in the park, they are mistaken.

Squirrels and Chipmunks

A variety of squirrels and chipmunks are present in Yosemite. Most visitors, particularly campers, will encounter one or more species of these active rodents.

The common squirrels are the western gray squirrel (all gray with a long bushy tail, often seen in trees), the Sierra chickaree (a reddish tree squirrel that chews on pine cones and squeaks a lot), the golden-mantled ground squirrel, and the California ground squirrel (a brown animal, speckled with white, which lives in burrows in the ground). The California ground squirrel is widespread throughout the state. The ones in Yosemite tend to be grayer than their counterparts in San Francisco. At higher elevations, the common ground squirrel is the "picket pin" (or Belding ground squirrel), which when

Chipmunk

seated in its erect posture looks like a stake driven into the ground.

There are at least five different species of chipmunks in the park. They are generally reddish brown in color, smaller than the squirrels, and wear four light-colored stripes separated by dark on their backs. These chipmunks are remarkably animated and quick. They dig burrows in stumps or the ground that are very hard to find.

A marmot on top of Half Dome

Marmot

A common sight in the park's higher elevations is the yellow-bellied marmot; watch for these rotund fellows at Olmsted Point on Tioga Road. Actually members of the squirrel family, marmots resemble woodchucks, for which they are sometimes mistaken. They regularly sun themselves on subalpine rocks. They behave tamely at certain roadside turnouts. Please do not feed them.

Marmots are about 15 to 18 inches long and weigh about 5 pounds. They are yellowish brown, live in dens under rock piles or tree roots, and hibernate during the winter. Their shrill warning note is distinctive.

Bighorn Sheep

Native to the Yosemite area, Sierra Nevada bighorn sheep were eliminated here around 1900 as a result of hunting and diseases spread by domestic animals.

In 1986 a herd of bighorns was released in the Tioga Pass area of Yosemite in an effort by scientists and researchers to reestablish a viable population. To date the experiment has been a success. Additional transplants have augmented the herd, which has been able to reproduce and survive on its own.

Bighorn sheep are remarkable rock climbers, able to ascend and descend amazingly steep terrain. Some sheep weigh up to 200 pounds and are three feet high at the shoulder. They are gray or buffy brown in color and grow hard, permanent horns. The males' horns sometimes spiral back into a full circle, while the females have small, slightly backward-curving horns. Watch for these beautiful animals in the mountainous regions around Tioga Pass.

Bighorn sheep

Because Yosemite plays host to over 240 different kinds of birds, it is not practical to provide an exhaustive bird list here. To learn more about Yosemite's birds, try a ranger-led bird walk or pick up a pair of binoculars and see what there is to see. The following highlights the species you are likely to encounter in the course of a visit.

Steller's Jay

This is one bird that just about everybody notices in Yosemite. The jay is bright blue with a dark head and a very prominent crest. Unfazed by humans, it boldly alights on tables and other perches close to food, all the while screeching its disagreeable screech. Surprisingly, the Steller's jay also is capable of producing a soft, warbling song. When a group of jays encounters a hawk or owl, the raucous cacophony of shrieks and calls that goes up is almost overpowering.

Acorn woodpecker

Acorn Woodpecker

In Yosemite Valley, the acorn woodpecker is the woodpecker you are likely to see. Colored black and white with a red head marking (sometimes there's yellow also), these industrious birds drill holes in trees, telephone poles, and buildings and fill them with acorns that they eat later (along with the bugs that have entered the acorns). Their flight is a distinctive series of shallowly U-shaped glides. They are exceptionally noisy, making a "wack-up, wack-up" call most often. Wherever you find oaks, you will find acorn woodpeckers.

Belted Kingfisher

Along the Merced River and other bodies of water in the park, this striking blue bird can be seen flying low or perched on branches and snags, watching for fish and aquatic insects. If you're lucky, one will plunge into the water and emerge with dinner in its beak. There is a noticeable crest and a reddish band on the chest. You'll know it's a kingfisher if you hear a loud, rattling, clicking call.

American dipper

American Dipper

Another water bird, the dipper, is truly phenomenal. Though gray and nondescript, these acrobatic creatures are named for their habit of bobbing up and down almost constantly. What's so phenomenal about them is their ability to fly into a stream or river and walk upstream, underwater, clinging to rocks on the bottom as they search for food. They have natural goggles—a translucent ocular membrane that covers their eyes while they hunt. As you stroll beside a stream or river, keep a close eye out for the amazing dipper!

Clark's Nutcracker

The high-country counterpart of the Steller's jay is the Clark's nutcracker. Also known as the "camp robber," this white, gray, and black bird with a prominent beak

Clark's nutcracker

has a harsh, cawing voice. Very conspicuous in areas around Tuolumne Meadows, the Clark's nutcracker does crack and eat pine nuts, but it is not averse to cleaning up around your campsite either. You'll see these birds typically above 9,000 feet.

Black-headed grosbeak

Black-headed Grosbeak

While picnicking or camping, you may see this other common Yosemite Valley resident. The grosbeak is characterized by its black, white, and orange markings and by its "gross beak" that is used for opening seeds. Oftentimes woods echo with the grosbeak's delightfully lyrical song, a rich warble. The black-headed grosbeak is a sure sign of spring.

Great horned owl

Great Horned Owl

You may never get a glimpse of this bird, but chances are good you will hear one. This nocturnal dweller in most of the park's life zones is active from dusk until dawn. Most of that time it issues a series of deep, sonorous hoots. If you happen to hear the horned owl, see if you can locate its perch. These owls are excellent ventriloquists, so don't be surprised if you fail. If you see a bird with large ear tufts, it's a sure sign you're looking at a great horned owl.

Peregrine falcon

Yosemite's Ten "Most Wanted" Birds

Serious birdwatchers (or "birders") often keep a list of every bird known to occur in North America and beyond, and when they see a bird they've never seen before, they will check it off this personal "life list." The goal is to see every single species on the list. There are several birds in Yosemite that are rarely seen or seen in few other places. These "most wanted" birds are feverishly sought by many zealous birdwatchers for their life lists.

1. Great gray owl
2. Gray-crowned rosy-finch
3. Peregrine falcon
4. Black-backed woodpecker
5. Flammulated owl
6. Northern goshawk
7. Pileated woodpecker
8. Williamson's sapsucker
9. Northern pygmy owl
10. Black swift

Lizards, frogs, and snakes are all members of this category. About forty different species of amphibians and reptiles are known to have established populations in the Yosemite Sierra, and there are no doubt more.

Amphibians (such as frogs and salamanders) lay their eggs in the water and breathe underwater through gills before reaching maturity, at which point they breathe air. Reptiles (such as snakes and lizards) breathe air.

Pacific tree frog

All of the lizards in Yosemite are harmless. Because they prefer warm locations, they are found primarily in the lower elevations of the park (Yosemite Valley and below). Most commonly seen is the western fence lizard. He's black or blotched brownish gray on top with a blue throat and belly.

At least fourteen different types of snakes inhabit the park. With the exception of the western rattlesnake, none are poisonous. The most regularly seen species is the garter snake, which frequents meadows, ponds, streams, and lakes (it's a remarkably good swimmer). The garter snake is black, gray, or dark brown with a cream-colored stripe down its back and usually has red blotches on its sides.

The rattlesnake is Yosemite's only venomous snake but rarely bites people. The rattler varies from cream to black in color with a variety of blotches. The head is broad, flat, and triangular, and when surprised, the snake will coil and shake the rattles it sports at the end of its tail. The result is a buzzing sound that is a warning to stay away. They're pretty rare above 5,000 feet.

Frogs and toads are abundant in Yosemite; there are a minimum of eight different kinds. You are more likely to hear from these denizens of the park than to see them. Most abundant is the Pacific tree frog, a small, green, gray, or brown fellow with a black mask and a constantly heard, year-round song. Recently it has been determined that the Sierra Nevada yellow-legged frog, once quite common, is in steep decline and may have disappeared from the park.

The last of the amphibians are the salamanders and newts. These small, slimy creatures like it moist and dark. That's why they're rarely seen. Most likely to be discovered is the California newt, the brownish orange newt that is often spotted after a heavy rain. Two species of salamander are found almost nowhere else but in the Yosemite region: the Mt. Lyell and the limestone salamanders.

Western fence lizard

Fishes

Despite the impression many people have that the Yosemite region is dotted with lakes and streams laden with native trout, there is only one game fish that naturally occurs in the park. That's the rainbow trout. There are five other native species, but they are relatively uncommon and are not game fishes (the Sacramento sucker, the Sacramento squawfish, the hardhead, the California roach, and the riffle sculpin).

When the glaciers moved through Yosemite during the last ice age, native fish populations were eliminated and most of the park's lakes and streams were left fishless. One job of the US Army in Yosemite National Park between 1890 and 1914 was to plant new fish species in the high country and provide greater opportunities for sport fisher-people. Non-native species that were introduced and now occur in the park are the cutthroat trout, the golden trout, the brown trout, and the brook trout. The brook and brown trout have

Brook trout

adapted best. This has been very unfortunate for the other animals that inhabit Yosemite's high lakes and streams. Trout are predators, and their sudden introduction has devastated these ecosystems.

For information about fishing in Yosemite, see page 89.

Rainbow trout

The Fishes of Yosemite National Park
("N" denotes a native species)

Trout
Brook trout
(*Salvelinus fontinalis*)

Brown trout
(*Salmo trutta*)

Cutthroat trout
(*Salmo clarki*)

Golden trout
(*Salmo aguabonita*)

Rainbow trout
(*Salmo gairdnerii*) N

Suckers
Sacramento sucker
(*Catostomus occidentalis*) N

Minnows
California roach
(*Hesperoleucus symmetricus*) N

Hardhead
(*Mylopharodon conocephalus*)N

Sacramento squawfish
(*Ptychocheilus grandis*) N

Sculpins
Riffle sculpin
(*Cottus gulosus*) N

The relatively undeveloped landscape of Yosemite Valley and the vast regions of wilderness around it are home to plants, animals, and other organisms that may in one way or another be hazardous to your health. The threat from these sources is generally not serious, and there are a number of precautions you can take and signs to watch for to avoid problems. Whatever you do, don't become frightened by the following list.

Giardia lamblia

This funny-sounding creature is a protozoan that causes an intestinal disease called giardiasis. Its symptoms are chronic diarrhea, abdominal cramps, bloating, fatigue, and weight loss. Because giardia has been found to be present in park lakes and streams, you should purify any drinking water that is not from the tap. Either boil it for three minutes, use an iodine-based purifier, or use a giardia-rated water filter.

Northern Pacific rattlesnake

Rattlesnakes

These wriggly reptiles are the only poisonous snakes in Yosemite. Out hiking, you will rarely encounter a rattler, and if you do it will almost always buzz its rattles when threatened. If you happen upon a rattlesnake, keep a safe distance and leave. Do not try to kill it or scare it away. It's always a good idea to watch carefully where you walk, where you put your hands, and where you sit.

Scorpions

In Yosemite's lower elevations, this threatening-looking insect hides by day and becomes active at night. The sting delivered by this scorpion is painful but not at all dangerous to humans. Sierran scorpions are quite different from the more serious desert scorpions found in places like Arizona. Scorpions hide under rocks and logs, so be cautious when you're lifting or rolling such objects.

Mosquitoes

These delightful insects have been characterized by one writer as the "most bothersome of the animal life in the High Sierra." Though relatively benign individually, roving bands of mosquitoes can make the lives of visitors, particularly in certain areas of the wilderness, totally miserable. They breed in locations with standing water, so they are common wherever there is snowmelt. Typically, that means 4,000 feet at the end of May advancing upwards to 10,000 feet by late July. What can be done about these pesky pests? Try repellents, long pants and long-sleeved shirts, and mosquito-net hats and tents. If you're backpacking, locate your camp to take advantage of any breeze and away from areas of moisture.

Ticks

Some park ticks, the small bugs that suck blood from a variety of mammals, carry an illness known as Lyme disease. Not every tick, however, is a carrier. Symptoms

Poison oak: leaves of three, let it be!

of the disease in its advanced form can include arthritis, meningitis, neurological problems, and cardiac problems. If it is detected early, treatment can cure or lessen the severity of the disease. If you think you might have been bitten by a tick, watch for a rash at the spot of the bite and for symptoms of the flu. If you contract Lyme disease and you believe its source was Yosemite, please call the Park Sanitarian at (209) 379-1209.

Poison Oak

This is one of the most widespread shrubs in California, and it's quite abundant in Yosemite's lower reaches. Fluids from the plant produce an irritating rash on the skin of humans and it can sometimes be very severe. Sufferers itch terrifically and can experience swelling. If you think you've been in poison oak, wash your body and clothes thoroughly to remove the oily fluid.

Spiders

There are a couple of interesting critters in this category. The single truly dangerous spider in Yosemite is the black widow. With its black, orb-shaped body featuring a red "hourglass" marking on its underside, this arachnid is easy to identify. The black widow is not aggressive, but when disturbed may bite and inject a nerve poison that can cause severe symptoms and even death. If bitten, see a physician quickly.

Much more fearsome in appearance is the tarantula, but this big, woolly fellow is fairly benign. Up to four inches across, tarantulas are active at night and don't bite unless provoked. The bite is painful but not dangerous. Relatively common in the foothills, they are rarely seen in the park.

Black widow

Peregrine falcon

While Yosemite National Park is abundant with varied plant and animal life, several indigenous species have been lost to extinction over the years, and threats to park life-forms persist despite the National Park Service's best efforts to protect them. Grizzly bears were once residents of the Sierra, and other birds, mammals, and plants have been lost as well.

Some species of plants and animals, though still present, have undergone local, state, or national declines, raising concerns about their possible extinction if protective measures are not implemented. The US Fish and Wildlife Service, California Department of Fish and Game, and Yosemite National Park have established categories for these species that reflect the urgency of their status and the need for monitoring, protection, and implementation of recovery actions.

Not all threats to park wildlife can be controlled. Take the peregrine falcon. These impressive flyers eat birds that migrate to Central and South America each winter. Use of pesticides is much more common in these wintering areas, and DDT has found its way into the systems of many Yosemite peregrines. The result is that their eggs became thin-shelled and subject to breakage. Nesting success dropped dramatically, and park officials feared that peregrines might be lost for good.

But through a fairly complicated augmentation procedure, the National Park Service has seen a growth in peregrine numbers and nests. During the nesting season, climbers were employed to reach peregrine nests and remove the fragile eggs. They were replaced with plastic phonies. Captive-raised chicks were later placed in the nests, and the parents adopted the newcomers without hesitation. Work continues to encourage other countries to limit their use of harmful chemicals.

Other significant programs have involved the restoration of meadows, oak woodlands, and other park areas. A number of revegetation efforts are underway to

The endangered Sierra Nevada bighorn sheep

reclaim portions of Yosemite that have been overused and stripped of plant life. Watch for evidence of this important work as you travel throughout the park, and be sure your use of Yosemite is consistent with the protection of the plants and animals here.

Sierra Nevada yellow-legged frog, an official candidate for both the federal and state endangered species lists

Bald eagle

Willow flycatcher

Yosemite Species Listed as At Risk by the US Government

Endangered
Sierra Nevada bighorn sheep

Threatened
Valley elderberry longhorn beetle

Plant Species of Concern
Bolander's clover
Congdon's lomatium
Slender-stemmed monkeyflower
Three-bracted onion
Tiehm's rock-cress
Yosemite woolly sunflower

Yosemite Species Listed as At Risk by the State of California

Endangered
Bald eagle
Great gray owl
Willow flycatcher

Threatened
Limestone salamander
Sierra Nevada red fox

Rare Plant Species
Congdon's lewisia
Congdon's woolly-sunflower
Tompkin's sedge
Yosemite onion

El Capitan and the Merced River

4 | Yosemite Valley

Yosemite Valley is truly the heart of the park. With its granite monoliths, towering waterfalls, and peaceful meadows, the valley is unique in the world for its remarkable scenery. Its seven square miles make up only a small fraction of the park's entire area, but 75 to 80 percent of the visitors to Yosemite spend their time there.

Not surprisingly, this results in crowded conditions on popular weekends and during the summer. Campgrounds fill, concessioner accommodations become completely reserved, and day users clog valley roads and parking lots. Efforts have been made to reduce the congestion caused by such heavy use, and some improvements have resulted. Among them are a one-way road system, the closure of roads to automobile traffic in the east end of the valley, development of an extensive network of bicycle paths, and the implementation of a shuttle bus system that links most developed areas in eastern Yosemite Valley.

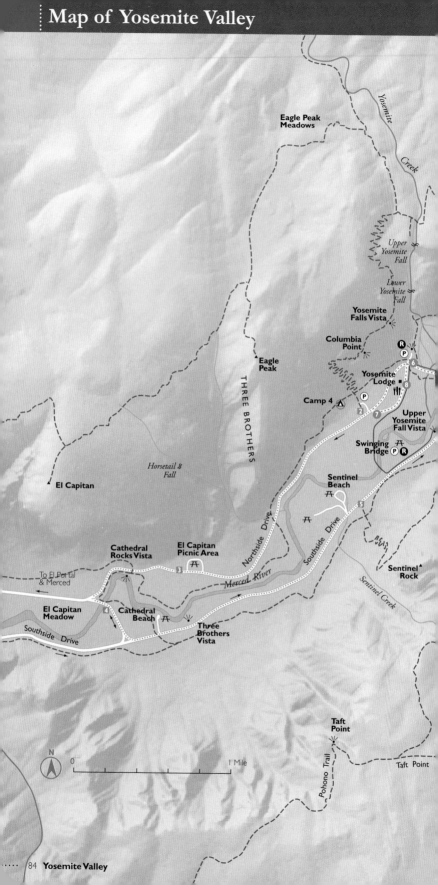

Map of Yosemite Valley

Eagle Peak
Meadows

Yosemite Creek

Upper
Yosemite
Fall

Lower
Yosemite
Fall

Yosemite
Falls Vista

Columbia
Point

R
P

6

Yosemite
Lodge

P
2   7

Camp 4

Upper
Yosemite
Fall Vista

Swinging
Bridge
P R

Sentinel
Beach

THREE BROTHERS

Eagle
Peak

5

Horsetail
Fall

El Capitan

Sentinel
Rock

Northside Drive

Southside Drive

Cathedral
Rocks Vista

El Capitan
Picnic Area

3

To El Portal
& Merced

Merced River

Sentinel Creek

El Capitan
Meadow

4

Cathedral
Beach

Three
Brothers
Vista

Southside Drive

Taft
Point

Pohono Trail

Taft Point

N

0   1 Mile

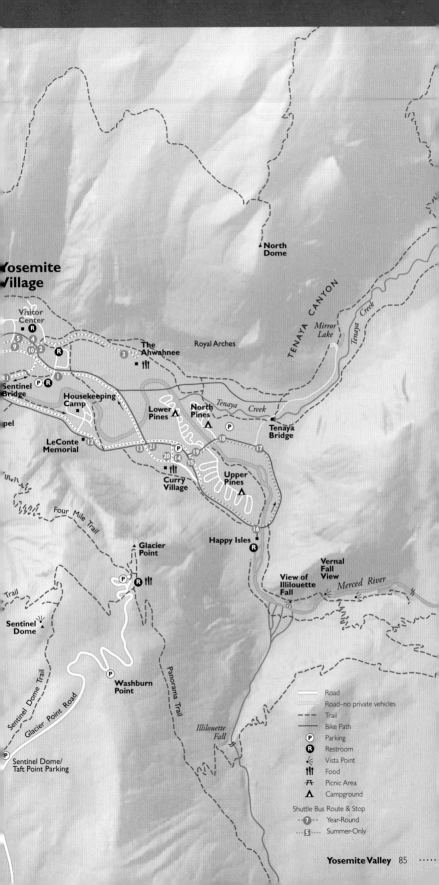

Yosemite Village

Visitor Center

The Ahwahnee

Royal Arches

North Dome

TENAYA CANYON

Mirror Lake

Tenaya Creek

Sentinel Bridge

Housekeeping Camp

Lower Pines

North Pines

Tenaya Creek

Tenaya Bridge

pel

LeConte Memorial

Curry Village

Upper Pines

Four Mile Trail

Glacier Point

Happy Isles

Vernal Fall View

View of Illilouette Fall

Merced River

Sentinel Dome

Trail

Washburn Point

Panorama Trail

Sentinel Dome Trail

Glacier Point Road

Illilouette Fall

Sentinel Dome/ Taft Point Parking

	Road
	Road–no private vehicles
	Trail
	Bike Path
P	Parking
R	Restroom
	Vista Point
♀♀♀	Food
⊼	Picnic Area
Λ	Campground

Shuttle Bus Route & Stop
- 7 - Year-Round
- 5 - Summer-Only

Can You Find the Visitor Center?

Lots of visitors come to believe, after hours of searching, that the Yosemite Valley Visitor Center has been purposely hidden from them. In many national parks, the first place you are directed to, by prominent signs, is the parking lot right smack in front of the visitor center. Not so in Yosemite Valley. Here you must either possess a doctorate in nuclear physics or have experience as a Green Beret to make your way to "Information Central."

The Yosemite Valley Visitor Center

It really is worth taking the time to find the visitor center, because it's the ideal place to start your visit. There you will find an impressive orientation film, information services provided by knowledgeable rangers, a complete bookstore, and excellent exhibits that cover Yosemite's natural and cultural history. Near the visitor center are an Indian Cultural Exhibit and Indian Village, plus the Yosemite Museum.

You can get to the visitor center by shuttle bus, on bicycle, or on foot. Here's how to manage it from selected valley locations.

From Day Visitor Parking (Camp 6)

Park your car and board one of the free "express" shuttle buses headed to the Yosemite Valley Visitor Center (bus stop 1). The bus stops in front of the visitor center (its only stop), then returns to the day visitor parking area. If you'd rather walk, there's a map available at the information station there that will guide you. It's about a one-third-mile walk.

From the Pines Campgrounds

Jump on a shuttle bus at the stop nearest to you (bus stops 15, 16, and 21 are all close) and disembark at Yosemite Valley Visitor Center (bus stop 5). The visitor center is 50 yards from the bus stop, on your right.

From Housekeeping Camp

The shuttle bus stops right in front of the entrance to the camp (bus stop 13). Take it and get off at Yosemite Valley Visitor Center (bus stop 5). The visitor center is 50 yards from the bus stop, on your right.

From the Ahwahnee Hotel

It's about a fifteen-minute walk along the Ahwahnee Meadow and past the Church Bowl to the visitor center. Or take the free shuttle bus from in front of the hotel (bus stop 3) and get off at the visitor center (bus stop 5).

Ribbon Fall

El Capitan

THREE BROTHERS

Col

Ca

Sentinel Beach

El Capitan Picnic Area

Cathedral Rocks Vista

Northside

3

Merced Riv

Southside Dr

Big Oak Flat Road To Tioga Road & Manteca via (120)

Rainbow View

rockslides

El Capitan Vista

El Capitan Meadow

Three Brothers Vista

Pohono Bridge

Valley View

Arch Rock Road To El Portal & Merced via (140)

P Tunnel View

P R

Bridalveil Fall

Cathedral Beach Picnic Area

Bridalveil View

Cathedral Rocks

To Glacier Point, Wawona, Oakhurst & Fresno via (41)

Stanford Point

Bridalveil Creek

N

0   1 M

Dewey Point

From Yosemite Lodge

Catch the free shuttle bus in front of the lodge registration area (bus stop 8). It will drop you off a few yards from the visitor center's front door (bus stop 9). The walk from Yosemite Lodge to the visitor center is less than a mile, flat and easy, and affords lots of good views along the way.

From the Parking Area behind the Village Store

Walk around or through the Village Store to the pedestrian mall on the other side of it. Turn to your right and walk approximately 200 yards up the mall to the visitor center, which is located at the mall's west end. If you're on your bicycle, follow the well-marked bike trails and watch for signs directing you to Yosemite Village and the visitor center.

Free Shuttle Bus Rides

The easiest way to get around in Yosemite Valley (and to get out of your car and avoid traffic) is to ride, free of charge, the Yosemite Valley shuttle bus system. With stops at just about all locations in the eastern end of the valley (and a stop at El Capitan in summer), the buses run every ten minutes or so (somewhat less frequently in the winter) and access areas such as Happy Isles and Mirror Lake that are closed to private automobiles. In winter, shuttle service to several stops may be discontinued. Check in at the Yosemite Valley Visitor Center to find out which stops are working.

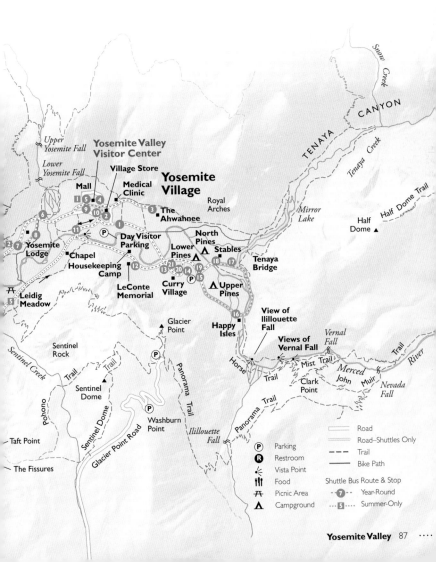

Lee Stetson as John Muir

John Muir in Person

Noted actor Lee Stetson regularly portrays John Muir in dramatic presentations in Yosemite Valley. It's Yosemite Theater at its best. See page 90.

A Browse through the Ansel Adams Gallery

This classy shop has been a leading Yosemite establishment since 1902. If you're a photographer, consider this your headquarters in the park. See page 52.

The Hike to Vernal Fall

An amazingly popular trip, and for good reason. The short, strenuous hike is essential Yosemite: rock, light, and water at their most spectacular. See page 92.

A Seat at Bracebridge Dinner

This lavish Christmas pageant is held annually at the Ahwahnee Hotel and features delicious food, seasonal music, elaborate costumes, and festive decorations. See page 23.

Breakfast at the Ahwahnee

It's a delight any time of the year to start your day with a casual yet luxurious breakfast in the Ahwahnee's grand dining room. See page 99.

The Panorama from Tunnel View

This classic Yosemite viewpoint never ceases to amaze. From this spot the valley's geologic origin couldn't be more evident. See page 101.

A Visit to the Visitor Center Bookstore

Nowhere else in the universe has such a complete collection of books and other materials related to Yosemite and the Sierra Nevada been assembled in one place. See page 86.

Lower Yosemite Fall in Springtime

When the snows of the Yosemite high country begin to thaw, the Yosemite Falls are revitalized. Liquid thunder! See page 92.

Vernal Fall and the Mist Trail

Enjoy an Interpretive Program

Throughout the year, park interpretive rangers and others present a wide variety of programs, walks, demonstrations, campfires, slideshows, films, and talks. There is usually no charge for these activities. Occasionally reservations are required. Consult the *Yosemite Guide* for the daily schedule of these programs.

Visit Yosemite Valley's Eastern End

The free shuttle bus route takes visitors to the area of Yosemite Valley that is no longer accessible by private automobile. Happy Isles (the trailhead for hikes to Vernal and Nevada falls and Half Dome) and Mirror Lake can only be reached by the shuttle bus or on bicycle or by foot. Excellent views of many landmarks, including Glacier Point, Half Dome, Tenaya Canyon, and Washington Column, are afforded from stops along the way. This section of the shuttle bus route may be closed in winter.

Make a Circle Tour of the Entire Valley

Many of the park's most famous spots, such as El Capitan, Bridalveil Fall, Tunnel View, Cathedral Rocks, and Sentinel Rock, are in west valley locations. Shuttle service to El Capitan is available in summer, but at other times of year you may want to take a self-guided circle tour. Use the *Yosemite Road Guide* to develop your own route. It's packed with interesting information and facts that will enhance your experience. The park concessioner, DNC, offers a two-hour guided tour in an open-air tram that visits most of the picturesque spots in Yosemite Valley. Check at the front desks of the various lodging facilities or behind the Village Store for tour details and prices.

Take a Bicycle Ride

Whether you've brought your bicycle or not, you can still see Yosemite Valley on two wheels. Bicycle rentals (with helmet) can be arranged all year at Yosemite Lodge, (209) 372-1208, and summer only at Curry Village, (209) 372-8319. More than eight miles of paved bicycle paths separate bicycle traffic from autos, and bicycling is especially good on the closed sections of roadway in the valley's east end. Try to avoid bicycling on busy valley roads that are often flooded with automobiles. As a rule, distracted, sightseeing drivers are not particularly attentive to bicyclists. Apart from that, there are some fairly strict rules for bicycle use in the valley:

- Bicyclists should stay on paved bike paths and roads.

- No riding on walking trails and into meadows. Erosion and vegetation damage will result otherwise.

- Mountain and all-terrain bicycles are permitted in Yosemite Valley but not allowed on unpaved surfaces. Check at the Yosemite Valley Visitor Center for appropriate mountain bike routes.

- Ride to the right in single file.

Catch a Fish

There are lots of trout in Yosemite Valley, but the Merced River is heavily fished. Stocking of trout is no longer done, and resident lunkers have developed a wariness of people and their multifarious fishing devices. Nevertheless, nice fish are caught every season by anglers of every skill level. Fishing in Yosemite is allowed in streams and rivers from the last Saturday in April to November 15. Fishing is allowed year-round in park lakes and reservoirs. On the Merced River in Yosemite Valley, only catch-and-release fishing is allowed for rainbow trout. No natural or organic bait may be used, only artificial lures and flies with barbless hooks. The limit is five per day with ten in possession. California fishing licenses are required (16 years of age and over) and may be purchased at the Village Sports Shop and at the Wawona Store. On the Merced River just outside the park, between the boundary and downstream to the Foresta Bridge, fishing is allowed all year but only with artificial lures with barbless hooks, with a minimum size limit of 12 inches total length and a maximum daily bag limit of two. Consult California Fish and Game regulations for further Yosemite fishing rules.

Paint a Picture

Free outdoor art classes are available during most parts of the year at the Yosemite Art Center. Artists working in many different media offer hands-on learning experiences to interested students regardless of skill level. Located on the Village Mall south of the Village Store near bus stop 2, the Yosemite Art Center is cosponsored by the National Park Service, the Yosemite Conservancy, and DNC Parks & Resorts at Yosemite. Class sessions are four hours in length and are scheduled from early spring through October and during holiday periods.

Ride 'Em Cowboy

Horseback rides are offered (for those with hardened backsides) by DNC Parks & Resorts at Yosemite from their stable in the east end of Yosemite Valley (bus stop 18). Guided trips in two-hour, half-day, and full-day lengths are given to such destinations as Nevada Fall and Glacier Point. For reservations and information call 372-8348 between 7:30 a.m. and 5 p.m.

Rafting the Merced River

Get Your Head Wet

The Merced River provides miles of beaches and numerous refreshing swimming holes during the summer months (it's too cold and fast-flowing in the spring). Or try out Mirror Lake. If you must swim in a heated pool, in summer there's one at Yosemite Lodge and another at Curry Village. A small pool is available only for guests at the Ahwahnee Hotel. Don't swim above the waterfalls!

Indulge the Kids

The Nature Center at Happy Isles (near bus stop 16) is a great spot for parents and their children, open from spring until October (check the *Yosemite Guide*). You can purchase workbooks for the Junior Ranger and Little Cub programs, and there are exhibits of park animals, a children's corner, a night display, and much more. Kids can check out, free of charge, an "Explorer Pack"—a convenient-to-carry daypack filled with guidebooks and activities for the whole family. There are packs available on different topics, including "Small Wonders," "Tree Trivia," and "Rocking in Yosemite."

Go for a Hike

There's a price to be paid for Yosemite Valley's towering cliffs and sheer walls. Practically every hike leading out of Yosemite Valley is straight up and strenuous! But the valley floor offers many enjoyable walks over flat terrain, and no matter what your hiking ability, you can find a trail to suit you. Several trails on the Yosemite Valley floor are wheelchair accessible. When you hike, be sure to wear sturdy, comfortable shoes and clothes that allow freedom of movement. Carry a flashlight and raingear. Rain (or snow) is a possibility in every season. Don't forget plenty of water (drinking from streams and rivers is not advised) and lunch and snacks. Dogs on leashes are allowed on fully paved trails on the floor of Yosemite Valley, but nowhere else.

Take in the Yosemite Theater

Throughout the year, dramatic and musical performances are offered by the Yosemite Theater program. Designed to supplement the interpretive activities of the National Park Service, Yosemite Theater is sponsored by the Yosemite Conservancy. Modest fees are charged for the various presentations. Best known of the theater programs are Lee Stetson's one-man stage productions in which he portrays John Muir. Also popular is the award-winning film *Return to Balance, a Climber's Journey*, which is presented by climber Ron Kauk and filmmaker Sterling Johnson. Programs for every taste include musical campfire programs and slide and film presentations. Tickets for the performances may be purchased at the Yosemite Valley Visitor Center.

Hear a Lecture

Each summer the Sierra Club operates the LeConte Memorial Lodge, an educational center and library located across from Housekeeping Camp at bus stop 12. The Sierra Club built the lodge in 1903 in honor of Joseph LeConte, eminent University of California geologist. Berkeley architect John White designed the Tudor-style, rough-hewn granite building. Most evenings, special lectures are presented here free of charge to interested visitors and Sierra Club members. Consult the *Yosemite Guide* or visit the LeConte Lodge for a schedule.

Saunter in the Cemetery

Fascinating insights into Yosemite's history can be gained from a visit to the Yosemite Cemetery, located across the street from and just west of the Yosemite Museum. Several significant figures from the park's past are buried here, including a number of Native Americans. First laid out in the 1870s, the cemetery houses the graves of such persons as James Mason Hutchings, Galen Clark, James Lamon, Sally Ann Castagnetto, Suzie Sam, and Lucy Brown. An informative publication, "Guide to the Yosemite Valley Cemetery," is on sale at the Yosemite Valley Visitor Center. If you do visit the cemetery, remember that it is a sacred place for many and that proper respect should be shown.

Accessibility

Many programs, facilities, and trails in Yosemite Valley (and throughout the park) are suitable for visitors in wheelchairs, with assistance. Also available are: assistive listening devices for programs, audio tours for the blind, many tactile exhibits, sign language interpreters (summer only), and a Braille brochure on Yosemite. Brochures are also available in German, French, Italian, Chinese, Japanese, Korean, and Spanish. Information on accessible park programs, facilities, and trails can be found at park entrances or information stations or online, where the "Yosemite Accessibility Guide" can be downloaded: http://www.nps.gov/yose/planyourvisit/upload/access.pdf.

Visit the Wilderness Center

Located in the small building between the Ansel Adams Gallery and the post office, the Wilderness Center offers a number of informative displays, a great relief map of the entire park, information on planning your own trip into the wilderness, and maps, guidebooks, and selected backpacking items. It's also the place to pick up wilderness permits, make wilderness reservations (see page 17), and rent bear-resistant food canisters.

Pack a Picnic

There are a number of fine spots for a picnic in Yosemite Valley. In the eastern end of the valley, ride the shuttle bus to Happy Isles or take the walk to Mirror Lake. To the west, try El Capitan picnic area (on the right side of Northside Drive about two miles west of Yosemite Lodge),
Bridalveil Fall parking area (intersection of the Wawona Road and Southside Drive), Cathedral Beach picnic area (on the left side of Southside Drive just past the El Capitan crossover), Sentinel Beach picnic area (on the left a mile or so farther along Southside Drive), or Swinging Bridge picnic area (less than half a mile farther, on the left). See the map on pages 86-87 for locations. Please make sure that you leave your picnic site as you found it and pack out all your waste, even watermelon seeds and apple cores. You may not eat these, but animals will.

Ranger Shelton Johnson

Enjoy an Outdoor Adventure

Throughout the year, the Yosemite Conservancy presents a series of outdoor adventures in Yosemite Valley and at other park locations. Some of the courses, covering such topics as botany, geology, natural history, photography, art, and backpacking, are offered for college credit. Programs have been designed for all levels of experience and for every type of Yosemite user. The instructional staff is excellent. For a catalog of classes or more information, call the Yosemite Conservancy at (209) 379-2321, visit www.yosemiteconservancy.org, or write: Yosemite Outdoor Adventures, Box 230, El Portal, CA 95318.

The floor of Yosemite Valley is criss-crossed with many trails, and paths hug the base of both the north and south valley walls. From about any point, there's good hiking. Wherever you walk, be sure it's not on one of the main roadways. Get out of your car and explore some of Yosemite's less-developed locales. You'll be amply rewarded for your effort.

Mirror Lake

Take the free shuttle bus to the Mirror Lake Junction (bus stop 17; see page 87). During the winter you may have to walk from the Pines campgrounds (bus stop 19). From this point it's a relaxing half-mile saunter over pavement to Mirror Lake. The trail beyond is also gentle as it follows Tenaya Creek eastward and then circles back. Walking up Tenaya Creek adds about 3 miles to the total distance. Views of Half Dome, Mt. Watkins, and Basket Dome are superb.

Mirror Lake

Vernal Fall Bridge

This special vantage point is reached from Happy Isles (bus stop 16; see page 87). You may need to walk from Curry Village during the winter, when the shuttles may not run this way. Undoubtedly the most popular and busiest hike in Yosemite (you'll be elbow to elbow with lots of other people), the John Muir Trail leads seven-tenths of a mile to a bridge that allows a breathtaking view of Vernal Fall. The trail, while paved with asphalt, is not as easy as the other two hikes listed here. There is a moderate slope most of the way to the bridge, and there are a few ups and downs. But it's definitely worth the effort. If you're a strong hiker and still feeling hardy, the remaining hike along the Mist Trail to the top of the fall is about a half-mile. Be warned, however, that it's all straight uphill over a very steep trail and a large number of granite steps. It's called the Mist Trail because it leads along the right flank of Vernal Fall, which, particularly in spring, blows heavy mist over trail and hiker alike. It can be like a monsoon. Most people wear raingear, but even so, on this trail getting drenched is part of the adventure.

Lower Yosemite Fall

Walk, bicycle, or ride the shuttle bus to the Lower Yosemite Fall trailhead near Yosemite Lodge (bus stop 6; see page 87). It's no more than a quarter-mile to the base of the lower fall and its boisterous, watery display (at least most of the year). This, too, is a very popular excursion. If you continue over the bridge and follow the trail, you will loop back to the trailhead in less than a half-mile. On full-moon nights in April and May, take this walk and watch for beautiful "moonbows" in the lower fall—a phenomenon first written about by John Muir. You will have to check on the timing and location of the moonrise to get the full moonbow experience. It's worth staying up late (or getting up early) to see this spectacle.

Each of the major trails to the valley rim is very strenuous and requires an uphill hike of at least 3.5 miles over dozens of switchbacks. Be sure you possess the requisite time, energy, footwear, and physical condition before you set off on any of these hikes. Also be sure to check the weather and to turn back early if rain clouds appear—even at a distance.

Lower Yosemite Fall

Yosemite Falls Trail

This climb up the sheer north wall pays off with remarkable views of the falls and Yosemite Valley generally. The trail leaves from behind Camp 4, across from Yosemite Lodge. The 3.6-mile route gains 2,700 feet in elevation as it passes Columbia Point, the top of Lower Yosemite Fall, and finally leads to the brink of Upper Yosemite Fall. When you reach the top, head back south toward the rim and find the walk down to the pipe railings. At this lookout, water leaps from the rock and braids itself into impressive patterns below you. Be sure to stay behind the railings—it's a long way down the waterfall. Allow six to eight hours for the round trip. Strong hikers should consider continuing on to Yosemite Point or Eagle Peak (see page 100).

The Four-Mile Trail to Glacier Point

Perhaps most disappointing to hikers on this route is that the Four-Mile Trail is almost five miles long (somebody rounded off a little too liberally). It's also an awful lot of work carrying yourself up 3,200 feet only to be greeted by automobiles, lots of people, and a snack bar. But the views from Glacier Point are sensational and all the more satisfying for the exertion. The trailhead is on the right, below Sentinel Rock on Southside Drive and about a mile before Yosemite Village. To drive to it you must make a loop on the valley's one-way road system, crossing over at El Capitan (watch for signs returning you to Yosemite Village). One of the earliest trails built in the valley, its location below and along the south wall means that it holds snow longer and opens later than the other trails, but also that it is cooler and shadier in the heat of July. This hike requires from six to eight hours up and back.

Tenaya Zigzags/ Snow Creek Trail

This is a less-used 3.5-mile route to the rim that actually originates in Tenaya Canyon, just east of Mirror Lake about 2.5 miles from bus stop 17. It affords stunning views of the canyon, including Clouds Rest and Quarter Dome and, directly across from you as you ascend, of Half Dome. Once you've hiked the 108 switchbacks to the rim, the closest promontory is North Dome, which is another 3 miles (see page 100). If North Dome is your destination, allow eight to ten hours round trip. The trailhead is at Mirror Lake, reached by taking a shuttle bus to the Mirror Lake junction (bus stop 17) and hiking a half-mile to the east. From the lake, the trail takes off to the north, up the canyon for a mile and a half, and then turns left up the cliff.

Vernal and Nevada Falls Trails

The walk to Vernal Fall over the Mist Trail is covered in the "Easy Hikes" section (previous page), but the trail continues on to Nevada Fall above. Two different segments of the route lead to the same place—one primarily for horses and one exclusively for people. The John Muir Trail takes off just past the Vernal Fall Bridge and is less steep, though longer (3.5 miles to Nevada Fall). The Mist Trail (foot traffic only) continues on past the top of Vernal Fall about a mile and a half over switchbacks to the rim. Ascending a gully to its left, hikers are treated to the world-famous profile view of Nevada Fall. From the top of the fall, trails lead to Little Yosemite Valley and Half Dome, and to Glacier Point over the Panorama Trail. Depart from Happy Isles (bus stop 16) and give yourself six to eight hours for the round trip.

Climbing Half Dome before the cables

For many the summit of Half Dome represents a hiking challenge they can't resist. For all its allure, the trip is long (about 17 miles round trip), steep (4,900 feet of elevation gain), and physically demanding. It's rewarding, too, particularly the incredible views both along the way and at the top. The last 200 yards up the back of the dome are steep enough to require the use of steel-cable handrails. Not for the faint of heart! Hold tight and keep moving.

If it sounds like too much of a grunt for one day, consider spending the night in Little Yosemite Valley (you'll need a wilderness permit) and make the ascent when you're fresh the next morning.

This busy trail (someone estimated that about seven hundred people scale Half Dome daily during the summer) begins from Happy Isles (bus stop 16). Allow ten to twelve hours minimum for the round trip.

Due to overcrowding on the trail, permits are now required to hike Half Dome, but changes may be in the works. For up-to-date information, check http://www.nps.gov/yose/planyourvisit/halfdome.htm. To get a permit (plan ahead!), visit www.recreation.gov or call (877) 444-6777.

Half Dome from the northeast

Valley Camping and Regulations

There are about 415 campsites in Yosemite Valley, most of them on the Recreation.gov system. Despite the fact that many of the campgrounds are practically void of vegetation and that campers are closely packed, these campsites are immensely popular. After all, it's Yosemite Valley.

It was in response to this popularity that the strictly structured reservation system was developed. While the need to reserve in advance does discourage spontaneity, it allows visitors coming from all over the US and the rest of the world to expect, with some certainty, that they will find a place to camp when they arrive. See page 15 for information on making a reservation.

For campers without reservations who find themselves in Yosemite Valley, there is a campground office at the north side of the parking area at Curry Village. Occasionally campsites become available due to cancellation, but to obtain one of them requires standing in line, sometimes for long periods of time; these sites are very limited and nearly impossible to obtain. You must put your name on a waiting list at the Curry Village campground reservation office as early in the day as possible.

Camping Regulations

Camping Limits

From May 1 through September 15, there is a seven-day camping limit in the valley. It extends to thirty days between September 16 and April 30. Thirty total camping days per calendar year are permitted in the park (the "no homesteading" rule). A maximum of six people is allowed in each campsite.

Check-out Time

Campsites must be vacated by noon on the day of departure. Check-in time is also noon, and sites may not be occupied before that time.

Bears

Yosemite Valley and other park locations provide excellent bear habitat. Bears are attracted by the same foods many campers enjoy—marshmallows, hot dogs, watermelon, etc. You are foolish if you do not store your food properly in your campsite (it's also a federal law). All of the valley campgrounds feature bear-proof food lockers measuring 45"w x 18"h x 34"d that are very effective. Keep your bear locker closed and latched at all times. Food is not allowed in any parked vehicle after dark, and there is a fine of up to $5,000 for improper food storage. Remove all trash from your campsite and place it in animal-resistant trashcans or dumpsters.

Pets

You may camp with your pets only in designated campgrounds. Pets must be on leashes (no longer than six feet) at all times, should never be left unattended, and are not permitted on trails off the floor of Yosemite Valley or any unpaved or semi-paved trails.

Hookups

There are no recreational vehicle utility hookups in the park. Electrical extension cords may not be connected to campground restroom outlets. Sneaky, but no cigar.

Campfires and Firewood

Collection of firewood of any kind (including dead and down wood) in Yosemite Valley is strictly prohibited. This regulation is the first step towards eliminating campfires, which have contributed to serious air-quality problems in the valley. (It's also aimed at making people smell less smoky.) Campfires are permitted only between 5 p.m. and 10 p.m. Firewood can purchased from the concessioner. Do not bring firewood into the park from other areas as such wood may be infested with microbial pests. Please use established fire rings and grates, and start your campfire with newspaper, not pine needles or cones. Use of chain saws is not permitted in the park.

Camping at nightfall in Yosemite Valley

Vehicle Parking

Only two vehicles are allowed per site. All of your vehicles, including tent and utility trailers, must be parked on the parking pads. You can't just drive into your campsite. If you have more than two vehicles, you must park any extras outside the campground. The maximum length for recreational vehicles is 40 feet.

Dump Stations

No wastewater of any kind should be drained onto the ground. That's gross. Use utility drains at campground restrooms for dishwater and other gray water. Use the dump station at Upper Pines Campground for RV and other septic tanks.

Quiet Hours

Campers are expected to maintain quiet between 10 p.m. and 6 a.m. Quiet generators may be used sparingly during the daytime. Or not at all, if I'm camped next to you.

Showers

Unfortunately, there are no shower facilities in any park campgrounds. In Yosemite Valley, showers are available for a fee at Curry Village and at Housekeeping Camp.

Laundry

There is a public laundromat at Housekeeping Camp.

Valley Campgrounds

The following campgrounds are located at an elevation of 4,000 feet in the eastern end of Yosemite Valley. Most require reservations (see page 15) and have a nightly fee of $20 per site (unless otherwise indicated). Some creative person decided to include "pines" in the name of practically every valley campground, so be sure to take note of the location you've been assigned, or you may spend hours trying to find your way home. As dates of operation are subject to variation, check with NPS for details.

North Pines

This set of 81 campsites is located adjacent to the stables and next to the Merced River. Both recreational vehicles and tents are accommodated here from mid-April through September. Pets allowed. Reservations required.

Upper Pines

The easternmost campground and the largest in Yosemite Valley, Upper Pines is closest to Happy Isles and the trail to Vernal and Nevada falls. There are 238 sites here, and some pets are permitted. Both RVs and tents are welcome, and a sanitary dump station is available. Open all year. Reservations required from March 15 through November.

Lower Pines

Lower Pines is across the river from North Pines, with several campsites near the banks of the Merced. The 60 campsites are available for both recreational vehicle users and traditional tent campers. Open approximately April through October. Pets allowed. Reservations required.

Camp 4

This campground is primarily for climbers and backpackers; traditional family campers would feel out of place here. Climbing headquarters for Yosemite Valley, Camp 4 attracts mountaineers from all over the world. It's located across from Yosemite Lodge on Northside Drive. Parking spaces are provided outside the camping area, and users must carry their equipment and food to their sites. The 35 campsites are communal in nature (six campers are assigned to each); the nightly fee is $5 per person. Campsites are available on a first-come, first-served basis. Be sure to arrive early because the campground fills up by midmorning practically every day of the summer. These campsites are not wheelchair accessible. Open for walk-in campers all year round; no pets are allowed.

Backpacker Walk-in

Designed for backpackers leaving for or returning from the backcountry (be prepared to show your wilderness permit), and also for bicyclists and bus passengers, this area of 25 sites has no parking. All access is by foot and there is a one-night maximum stay. Users should check in at North Pines Campground, where a ranger will provide directions. Open from April to October in a typical year. Campers are charged $5 per person per night on a first-come, first-served basis. No pets are allowed.

Gas

There are no longer any service stations in Yosemite Valley and gas is not available. The nearest gas to be pumped is in El Portal on Highway 140 (13 miles). There are also stations at Crane Flat on Big Oak Flat Road (15 miles), and in Wawona on Wawona Road (27 miles). Plan ahead and be sure you have plenty in the tank before you drive into the valley—gas in Yosemite is invariably expensive. A repair garage is open all year behind the Yosemite Village Store. A towing service is available 24 hours a day by calling (209) 372-8320.

Food: Restaurants

Though the cuisine is mostly American and waits can be considerable during the summer, there are plenty of places to eat in Yosemite Valley. The following is a location-by-location listing of valley eating establishments. Check the *Yosemite Guide* for hours of operation.

Yosemite Lodge

Food Court: Open for breakfast, lunch, and dinner year-round. Quick and perfect for families. Many different choices, plus a good coffee bar. Inexpensive.

The Mountain Room: Offering dinner only, daily from spring to fall, and on weekends and holidays in winter. This is Yosemite's "steakhouse," with other entrees including salmon and pasta. The Mountain Room offers lots of local, organic, sustainably produced meat and produce. The remodeled facility is very impressive, and the room offers remarkable views of the Yosemite Falls area from many tables. And it's one of the only places to dine outdoors in the summer. Open from 5:30 to 9:00 p.m. Moderate to expensive.

The Mountain Room Bar and Lounge: Besides beer, wine, and cocktails, this facility offers a la carte continental breakfast, and lunch featuring gourmet coffee, sandwiches, salads, yogurt, and a small selection of appetizers and entrees. Hours vary, but it's usually open from noon to 11 p.m. Inexpensive to moderate.

Yosemite Village

Degnan's Deli: Open year-round for sandwiches, soups, snacks, salads, and picnic items. They will build a sandwich to your specifications, and you can piece together a nice lunch basket. There are also some breakfast options. There's limited outdoor seating, so plan on making yours a moveable feast. Inexpensive to moderate.

Degnan's Fast Food and Ice Cream: Lunch and dinner selections, year-round. Fare includes hamburgers, chicken, frozen yogurt, and ice cream. Limited indoor seating, but a fairly large patio. Inexpensive.

The Loft: Serving lunch and dinner, spring to fall. Located upstairs at the east end of the Degnan's building, the Loft offers pizza, salads, and appetizers, with plenty of indoor seating. Moderate.

The Village Grill: Fast-food breakfasts, lunches, and dinners, spring to fall. Patterned roughly on a McDonalds menu (look for the Royal Arches?), offerings include burgers, chicken strips, sandwiches, shakes, and fries, with a morning menu of breakfast sandwiches and entrees. Located next to the Village Store with outdoor seating only. Inexpensive.

Curry Village

Curry Village Pavilion Buffet: For breakfast and dinner, spring to fall. Breakfast items include yogurt, cereal, fruit, baked goods, and hot entrees. For dinner there's soup, salad, pasta, hot entrees, stir-fry, taco bar, and desserts. A family favorite with inexpensive to moderate prices.

Hamburger Stand: Open spring to fall, this fast-food outlet has about the same offerings as the Village Grill. Hamburgers, chicken, fish sandwiches, chicken nuggets, salad, and soft drinks to go for consumption on the deck outside. Inexpensive.

Pizza and Bar: Open daily from spring to fall, this facility offers pizza and salad from 5 p.m. to 9 p.m. on weekdays, and from noon to 9 p.m. on weekends. Tables are outdoors on the deck. Inexpensive to moderate.

Taqueria: Open daily from spring to fall, this facility offers Mexican food from 11 a.m. to 5 p.m. Early and late in the season it only operates on weekends. Inexpensive to moderate.

Coffee Corner: For the caffeine-deprived; here you can find fresh-ground coffees, espressos, lattes, cappuccinos, fruit, baked goods, and boxed lunches. Located within the Curry Pavilion. Inexpensive.

Ice Cream: Open spring to fall, this small outlet offers sweet treats. It's located inside the Curry Pavilion at the Coffee Corner. Inexpensive.

The Ahwahnee

The Ahwahnee Dining Room: Breakfast, lunch, and dinner, year-round. This regal dining room is a true delight. It's a joy to behold its beamed ceilings and impressive chandeliers. Perhaps breakfast is the most enjoyable meal here; casual attire is allowed and one experiences a feeling of relaxation and elegance as daylight filters through the massive windows. Dinner is the traditional, formal meal at the Ahwahnee (though the views are obscured by darkness). Men must wear collared shirts and long pants, and reservations are suggested. The meals are superb, and like the Mountain Room, the Ahwahnee offers an impressive array of locally grown, sustainably produced foods. Call (209) 372-1489. Expensive.

The Ahwahnee Bar: Light fare and appetizers are served in the bar from noon to 10 p.m daily. Moderate.

Food: Groceries

Yosemite Valley contains four outlets for groceries and camp supplies. They are open year-round with the exception of the Housekeeping Camp store, which closes in winter. Check the *Yosemite Guide* for hours of operation, or call the indicated phone number.

Village Store

If you can't find it anywhere else in Yosemite Valley, come here. Of particular note are the butcher shop and the fresh produce. Located at the east end of the Village Mall at bus stop 2. Open from 8 a.m. to 9 p.m. (and sometimes later). Phone (209) 372-1253.

Degnan's Delicatessen

Degnan's Deli, included in the restaurant listings above, also has a decent selection of foodstuffs for picnics and snacks. West of the Village Store and next to the US Post Office on the mall. Open from 7 a.m. to 5 p.m. Phone (209) 372-8454.

Curry Village Camp Store

A general store with convenience items and gifts, located in the Pavilion building next to the Hamburger deck at Curry Village. Open from 8 a.m. to 7 p.m. Phone (209) 372-8325.

Housekeeping Camp Store

This is a convenience store catering to campers. It's open from spring to fall only, usually between 8 a.m. and 6 p.m. (and

sometimes later). Located at Housekeeping Camp near bus stop 12. Phone (209) 372-8333.

Lodging

The following is a list of lodging facilities, ranging from rustic to luxurious, in Yosemite Valley. Some rates are lower in winter, but overall there is little in the way of value lodging in the valley. Information on rates can be found at http://www.yosemitepark.com. For information on making reservations, see page 14.

Yosemite Lodge

Open all year, the lodge offers three types of accommodations: lodge rooms, standard rooms, and a few larger family rooms. Special value-season rates (both weekend and midweek) are available between November 1 and March 15. Yosemite Lodge is preferred to Curry Village in winter because of its warmer location. The lodge is situated near and offers pleasant views of Yosemite Falls and the Merced River. Besides the restaurants listed above, the following are available at Yosemite Lodge: gift shops, cocktail lounge, tour/activities desk, post office, outdoor amphitheater, swimming pool, bicycle rentals, and free shuttle service to various locations in the park. Moderate to expensive.

Camp Curry

Curry Village

Open from spring to fall and on holidays and weekends in winter. Originally designed to provide an economical lodging alternative in Yosemite Valley, Curry Village still features the least expensive accommodations. They are of three types: standard motel rooms with bath, cabins with bath, and canvas tent cabins without bath. Special value-season rates (both weekend and midweek) are available

The Ahwahnee Hotel

Other guest services available at the Ahwahnee are gift shops, a cocktail lounge, and a swimming pool for guests of the hotel only. Expensive.

Housekeeping Camp
The experience at Housekeeping Camp is somewhere between camping out and staying in a rustic cabin. Guests are provided a developed "campsite" that features a covered shelter, a cooking and dining area, cots, a table, and a fire ring. You must bring your own linen (or sleeping bags) and cookware. Call it luxury camping, if you prefer, which differs from staying in a Curry Village tent cabin because you are able to prepare your own meals. The camp is open from spring through fall only. Housekeeping Camp is located near the public campgrounds, across from LeConte Lodge, and adjacent to the Merced River.

The camp offers public showers, a store, and a laundromat. Inexpensive.

between November 1 and March 15. All cabins without bath utilize communal bathrooms. Curry Village is cooler in summer than other valley locations and is known for its informality. Nearby attractions are Happy Isles, the campgrounds, and the riding stable.

Other amenities include gift shops, showers, a mountaineering shop, a climbing school, swimming pool, an outdoor amphitheater, tour/activities desk, free shuttle service to various locations in the park, and bicycle and raft rentals, plus an ice rink in winter. Inexpensive to moderate.

The Ahwahnee
Ansel Adams called the Ahwahnee "one of the world's distinctive resort hotels." Open year-round, this grand and imposing hotel is definitely at the luxury end of the Yosemite lodging spectrum. Besides regular rooms in the main building, the Ahwahnee features several cottages on the grounds. Rooms and cottages all have bathrooms.

The hotel's Great Lounge is a study in high style (afternoon tea offers a relaxing respite), and the dining room (see page 98) is without parallel as an elegant setting for a meal. Located below the Royal Arches, the Ahwahnee offers fine views of Glacier Point and the valley's south wall.

The Ten Best Views from Above

Glacier Point

Not only does the point provide an overwhelming panorama, but it's accessible by car (for better or for worse). The commanding views of Yosemite's high country, Half Dome, the Yosemite, Vernal and Nevada falls, and the valley below are unequaled.

North Dome

This promontory allows the best view there is of Half Dome and Tenaya Canyon. Located on the north rim, it can be reached only by foot, either from Yosemite Valley (via the Yosemite Falls or Snow Creek trails) or from Tioga Road (via the Porcupine Creek trailhead near Porcupine Flat Campground). All routes are very strenuous. See pages 93, 130.

Eagle Peak

This lookout is actually the highest rock of the Three Brothers formation. About three miles by trail from the top of Yosemite Falls, the peak offers impressive views of the entire Yosemite region, the Sierra foothills, and the Coast Range far beyond.

Sentinel Dome

Lacking Glacier Point's glimpses of Yosemite Valley, this dome is almost a thousand feet higher. An unobscured, 360-degree vista presents itself to hikers who make the one-mile walk from the Glacier Point Road. Particularly spectacular under a full moon.

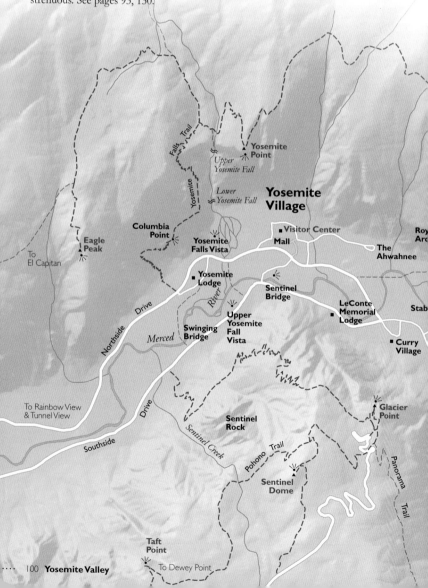

Tunnel View

While only partway up the southwestern rim of the valley, this viewpoint just below the Wawona Tunnel on Wawona Road is a Yosemite classic. More photos are shot at this location than anywhere else in the park, and for good reason. El Capitan, Bridalveil Fall, and Half Dome couldn't be more photogenic.

Half Dome

The only drawback of a perch here is that the view doesn't include Half Dome! Something seems missing from the landscape when you're sitting on this enormous rock that has come to symbolize Yosemite more than any other landmark. The eight-and-a-half-mile hike from Happy Isles is quite difficult, though hundreds of people a day undertake it each summer. See page 94.

Yosemite Point

About three-quarters of a mile to the east of the top of Yosemite Falls, the point is famous for its proximity to the Lost Arrow Spire, a remarkable freestanding shaft of granite. The view to the south rim is one of the best.

Dewey Point

The series of viewpoints along the Pohono Trail on the south rim of Yosemite Valley is special. Dewey Point can be reached over the McGurk Meadow trail that heads north from the Glacier Point Road near Bridalveil Creek Campground. Both Dewey Point and Crocker Point (a half-mile to the west) allow unusual perspectives on El Capitan and Bridalveil Fall. In winter, Dewey Point is a popular cross-country ski and snowshoe destination.

Rainbow View

This location is about a mile and a half up the rockslides trail that crosses the base of El Capitan. While the hike is a rough one over boulders, from the viewpoint roughly opposite the east end of the Wawona Tunnel one is sometimes treated to rainbow displays in Bridalveil Fall during midafternoons in summer.

Taft Point and the Fissures

Also on the Pohono Trail, these spots are accessed from the same trailhead on Glacier Point Road that heads to Sentinel Dome. An easy walk leads to Taft Point, with its view of the Cathedral Rocks and Spires and the north rim, and to the Fissures, which are deep clefts in the rock which drop hundreds of feet towards Yosemite Valley. Check out the echo here.

North Dome

To Snow Creek Trail

Tenaya Creek

Mirror Lake

Half Dome Trail

Half Dome

Little Yosemite Valley

Happy Isles

Vernal Fall

Mist Trail

Vernal Fall Bridge

John Muir Trail

Merced River

Nevada Fall

John Muir Trail

Road
Road—no private vehicles
Trail
View

N

0 — 1 Mile

Dogwood blossoms

5 South of Yosemite Valley

To the south of Yosemite Valley lies a part of the park that is less busy and noticeably more quiet. Known as the "Wawona District," the south end includes historic Wawona, the world-famous Mariposa Grove with its giant sequoias, and the road corridor that leads to Glacier Point. The main way to reach all of these locations is by car on Wawona Road, as only limited, seasonal shuttle bus service is available.

Map of South of Yosemite Valley

To Dewey Point

Glacier Point Road
closed beyond Badger Pass
from November–late May

To Yosemite
Valley

Glacier Point Road

Bridalveil

To Glacier Point,
Taft Point &
Sentinel Dome

Mono
Meadow

Badger Pass
Ski Area
(winter only)

Bridalveil
Campground

Chinquapin

Yosemite
West

Creek

Wawona Road

Yosemite National Park

Deer
Camp

South Fork Merced River

Alder Creek

Chilnualna Creek

Wawona Road

Chilnualna Fall

Wawona
Dome

Pioneer Yosemite
History Center

Falls Rd

Forest Drive

Wawona
Campground

Chilnualna

Wawona

Wawona Visitor Center
at Hill's Studio

Wawona
Hotel

**Sierra
National
Forest**

South
Entrance

Mariposa
Grove

N

0   2 Miles

41

Fish
Camp

To Oakhurst
& Fresno

Mount
Clark

Illilouette Creek

Illilouette Creek

Ottoway Lakes

Ostrander
Ski Hut

Ostrander Lake

BUENA VISTA CREST

Royal Arch Lake

Buena
Vista
Peak

Buck
Camp

Crescent Lake

Johnson Lake

Chain Lakes

South Fork Merced River

Road

Tram route

Trail

Ⓟ Parking

Ⓡ Restroom

Vista Point

Food

Picnic Area

Campground

Star Lakes

Sierra
National
Forest

Mount
Raymond

Iron
Mountain

The Mariposa Grove of Big Trees

No one comes away unimpressed by these towering sequoias. A world-class attraction. See page 113.

The Walk to Wawona Point

Quiet, little-visited, and offering a remarkable view, Wawona Point is the perfect destination for an excursion in the Mariposa Grove. See page 114.

The Outdoor Barbecue at the Wawona Hotel

On Saturday nights during the summer, enjoy a delicious meal on the lawn under the pine trees at this fine old hotel. Red-checked tablecloths in the wild. See page 111.

The Slopes at Badger Pass

Every winter, Badger Pass is transformed into a hotbed of skiing and snowboarding activity. Both downhill and cross-country opportunities abound. See page 22.

The Pioneer Yosemite History Center

Explore this collection of historic structures and take the horse-drawn stage rides that depart from the History Center and make a short loop to the Wawona Hotel. See page 110.

The View from Glacier Point

From the railing at Glacier Point, you are lord or lady of all the Yosemite you survey. The view is unforgettable. See page 115.

A Round at the Wawona Golf Course

Play nine holes at this exceptionally scenic and challenging course, or just take a walk once it has closed for the day. See page 110.

Ostrander Ski Hut in Winter

A strenuous nine-mile ski from Badger Pass south of Glacier Point Road, the hut offers shelter and warmth to wilderness skiers. See page 23.

The Mariposa Grove Museum

Wawona

Wawona is a historic community nestled on a beautiful meadow adjacent to the South Fork of the Merced River about twenty-seven miles south of Yosemite Valley. The area was settled very early in the park's history and became a stopover point on the stage route to the park. Galen Clark, a significant figure in Yosemite's past (see page 50), built Clark's Station there, and that cabin later grew to become the Wawona Hotel we know today.

To the east of the main road on both sides of the river, a large number of private cabins and homes have been developed. This area, known as Section 35, was held privately for many years before it became part of Yosemite National Park. Known as an "inholding," much of the tract is still largely privately owned, although the National Park Service has purchased several homes and lots. Many of the residences are available as summer rentals (see the "Lodging" section on page 118).

For those seeking information, directions, or help, there is a visitor center in Wawona. To find it, turn off Wawona Road into the Wawona Hotel grounds. The center is located within the Hill's Studio building, to the left of the fountain as you face the main hotel section. If there's no parking available, park near the store (just past the gas station) and follow signs up the hill to Hill's Studio. The phone number at the Wawona information station is (209) 375-9531.

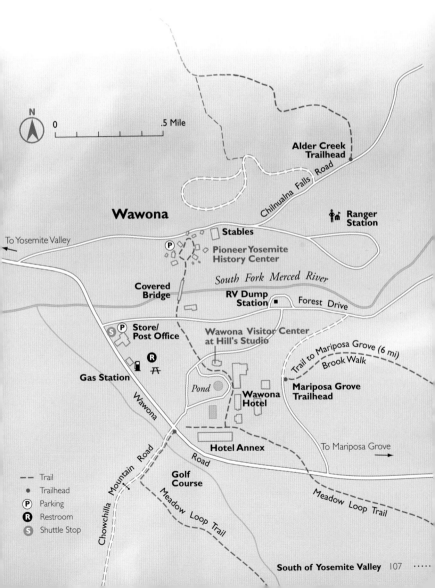

The Wawona Shuttle Bus

During the summer, a free shuttle bus operates in the Wawona area. Generally, the system runs from approximately May through September daily with stops at the Wawona Campground, the Wawona Store, South Entrance, and the Mariposa Grove of Big Trees. Check the *Yosemite Guide* for details, hours, and exact schedules.

But over the next five years, ill-advised investments in mining ventures and land purchases along with the completion of the Coulterville and Big Oak Flat Roads into Yosemite Valley spelled doom for Clark and Moore. They were forced to sell their lodging house and related properties to the Washburn Brothers in December 1874.

US Cavalry at Camp Wood, 1896

Wawona History

Though probably not deliberately, when Yosemite pioneer Galen Clark (see page 50) settled on 160 acres in Wawona in 1856, he selected a spot almost exactly halfway between Mariposa and Yosemite on the developing route for visitors. Clark seized the opportunity and built a rustic lodging house for travelers that was known as Clark's Station.

Though Galen Clark recognized the potential of his way station, he proved unable to fulfill it. His management of Clark's Station was poor, and he invested considerable funds in completing the Mariposa stage road to Wawona. Financial pressure forced Clark to take on Edwin Moore as a full partner in 1869, and all signs indicated that Clark's fortunes had turned.

The Washburns were an enterprising group of three brothers who had come to California from Putney, Vermont. They undertook a number of ventures in the Mariposa area before their purchase from Clark and Moore. It was their New England background that led them to cover the existing bridge over the South Fork of the Merced; it's the same bridge that leads into the Pioneer Yosemite History Center today.

At the same time they acquired the Wawona travelers' stop, the Washburns began work on the completion of the stage road from Wawona to Yosemite Valley. In this way they hoped to compete with the other routes. They finished the job in June 1875, and their plan began to meet with success.

In 1876 the Washburns put up the long white structure that stands just to the right of the main hotel building today.

And a year after the hotel burnt in 1878, the two-story structure that is still used as the main hotel building went up. The inn was known as Big Tree Station until 1882, when it officially became the Wawona Hotel. Additional buildings went up over the years.

Congress established Yosemite National Park in 1890 and directed that the US Army should be responsible for managing it. Because Yosemite Valley and the Mariposa Grove of Big Trees had already been granted to the State of California and were not part of the national park, locating park headquarters became a challenge. Because Wawona was one of the few developed areas within the new park (though not part of it), among other reasons, it was selected as the summer command for Army personnel.

Known as Camp A. E. Wood, headquarters were located on the site of the present Wawona Campground. For sixteen summers, cavalry troops from the San Francisco area occupied the camp and engaged in caring for the new park. Among their many activities were exploring and mapping, trail building, stocking fish, and enforcing anti-hunting and trespassing regulations. When the state grant and Yosemite National Park were combined in 1906, Camp A. E. Wood was abandoned and Army headquarters were relocated to Yosemite Valley.

Over the years, changes to Wawona generally came with changes in transportation. Following the completion of the Wawona Stage Road, the Washburns' stage company flourished and visitation grew. In 1914 automobiles first navigated the road between Wawona and Yosemite Valley. The Wawona Hotel management recognized that automobile travelers would want more recreational opportunities, and they proceeded to build a dance floor, soda fountain, croquet court, swimming tank, and golf course over the next fifteen years.

As the Wawona Hotel prospered, so did the community in Section 35 (the number assigned to the plot of land in its legal description), which included several homesteads and which housed workers for the hotel and for other support services. When most of the Wawona region was added to Yosemite National Park in 1932, only Section 35 remained in private ownership. It is in this area of Wawona that many private homes, cabins, and visitor rentals are located today (see page 118).

Stagecoach exiting the covered bridge in Wawona

The top of Chilnualna Fall

Step Back in Time

The Pioneer Yosemite History Center is a collection of historic buildings that have been moved from other locations within the park. The center is located near the Wawona Hotel, just east of the gas station (prominent signs will direct you there). Each building represents a different time period in Yosemite's history. At times during the summer, park rangers and volunteers engage in "living history," which

Ranger Burl Maier driving a stagecoach

means that they dress in period costume and portray actual Yosemite residents from bygone days. You can try, but you'll have a hard time getting these old-timers to break character.

Interesting attractions are an exhibit of old horse-drawn vehicles, the covered bridge over the South Fork built in the 1870s that has been restored, and a blacksmith who actually practices his craft while you watch.

For a small fee, you can take a short ride on a horse-drawn stage to get a feel for what early trips to Yosemite must have been like. During parts of the year, regular ranger-led tours of the History Center may be scheduled (consult the *Yosemite Guide* for details).

Hit the Links

A conspicuous adjunct to the Wawona Hotel is the beautifully laid-out golf course nearby. Whether you're a golfer or not, a stroll around the nine-hole circuit is both relaxing and replete with scenic vistas. (If you're a nongolfer, take your walk after the course is closed, please!)

The golf course was built in 1917 and features some of the most magnificent golfing holes anywhere. While the layout is not particularly long, it features lots of rough and water hazards and is remarkably challenging. Watch out for deer grazing the fairways, particularly on the first hole.

Golf clubs and carts are available for rent at the Golf Shop, and reserving a tee time is recommended. Phone (209) 375-6572.

Enjoy an Outdoor Barbecue

Every Saturday night during the summer, an old-fashioned barbecue is served outdoors on the expansive lawn of the Wawona Hotel. Red-checked tablecloths sport steaks, hamburgers, corn on the cob, western beans, and more. Check at the hotel desk for times and prices.

Get in the Swim

The South Fork of the Merced River as it runs through Wawona is dotted with swimming holes and beaches. Find a spot to put down your towel and cool off, or try your hand at fishing. (See page 89 for general fishing information and regulations.) Guests at the Wawona Hotel may use the small swimming pool on the grounds.

Horse around a Little

DNC Parks & Resorts at Yosemite maintains a riding stable in summer behind the Pioneer Yosemite History Center on Chilnualna Falls Road (about a quarter-mile off the main highway). Guided horseback or mule rides of varying lengths are offered. Stop by the stable for details or call (209) 375-6502 or visit http://www.yosemitepark.com/ Activities_MuleHorsebackRides.aspx.

Hike Some More

A variety of hiking awaits you at Wawona, from easy and flat to steep and strenuous. Be sure to check park hiking guidelines before you take off (see page 90). Give yourself plenty of time and don't undertake more than you're capable of.

Range with a Ranger

From spring through fall, a program of ranger naturalist activities is presented free of charge to the public in the Wawona area. Check the *Yosemite Guide* for listings and times.

Tour an Artist's Studio

The Thomas Hill Studio on the grounds of the Wawona Hotel is open in summer as a visitor center and features a terrific exhibit on the work of Hill along with other art programs. Thomas Hill used the building as a summer studio from 1885 until his death in 1908, and his fine landscape paintings of Yosemite and elsewhere are critically acclaimed.

Saddled mules ready for a ride

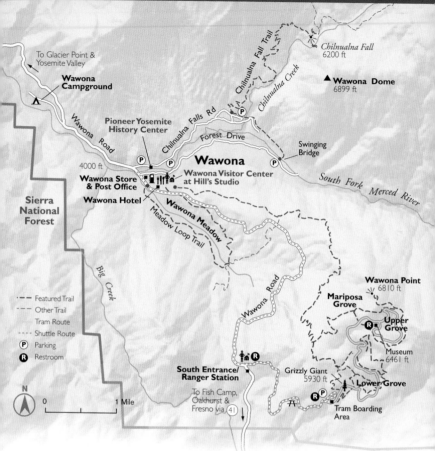

Map legend:
- Featured Trail
- Other Trail
- Tram Route
- Shuttle Route
- ℗ Parking
- ℞ Restroom

To Glacier Point & Yosemite Valley

Wawona Campground

Pioneer Yosemite History Center

Chilnualna Falls Rd

Chilnualna Fall Trail

Chilnualna Creek

Chilnualna Fall 6200 ft

▲ **Wawona Dome** 6899 ft

Wawona Road

Forest Drive

Wawona

4000 ft

Wawona Store & Post Office

Wawona Hotel

Wawona Visitor Center at Hill's Studio

Swinging Bridge

South Fork Merced River

Sierra National Forest

Wawona Meadow

Meadow Loop Trail

Big Creek

Wawona Road

Wawona Point 6810 ft

Mariposa Grove

Upper Grove

Museum 6461 ft

Lower Grove

Grizzly Giant 5930 ft

South Entrance/ Ranger Station

To Fish Camp, Oakhurst & Fresno via (41)

Tram Boarding Area

N — 0 — 1 Mile

The Meadow Loop

This pleasant walk begins directly across Wawona Road from the entry road to the Wawona Hotel. Follow the gravel road about 50 yards across the golf course just into the trees and take the road that leads off to the left. This almost entirely flat route skirts the edge of the Wawona Meadow and then circles back, crosses Wawona Road, and finishes up behind the Wawona Hotel. Approximately 3 miles total, the loop should take an hour and a half or less. The hike is easy, leisurely, and picturesque.

Chilnualna Fall

The trail to this delightful cascade is fairly strenuous, gaining almost 2,500 feet in approximately 4 miles. Start from the trailhead, which is located 1.7 miles east of the main road on Chilnaulna Falls Road. There's parking space on the right for 25 to 30 cars. If the road turns to dirt, you've gone too far. The route is an enjoyable one through manzanita, deer brush, and bear clover, and finally meets with Chilnualna Creek. The fall, instead of

leaping and free-falling from some precipice, drops through a narrow chasm in a furious rush. Allow six to eight hours for this 8-mile round trip. Start early in the morning, when temperatures are cooler, and carry lots of water in the summer, when the weather can be extreme.

Mariposa Big Trees

Starting behind the Wawona Hotel is a long, uphill climb to the Mariposa Grove of giant sequoias. Passing through forest most of the way, the trail offers excellent views of the Wawona Basin and Wawona Dome as it nears the big trees. The trail ends at the Mariposa Grove Museum in the Upper Grove near the fallen Tunnel Tree. Because the elevation gain is 3,000 feet in 6.5 miles, this hike is for the well-conditioned only. For an easier alternative, take the summer shuttle bus to the Mariposa Grove and hike back to Wawona. Figure on spending eight to ten hours making the up-and-back trip of 13 miles.

Activities at the Mariposa Grove of Big Trees

Located at the southernmost end of Yosemite, the Mariposa Grove is the largest stand of giant sequoias (*Sequoiadendron giganteum*) in the park. These ancient monarchs are inadequately described with numbers, but how else do you do it? Sequoias can be 3,000 years old, reach almost 300 feet into the sky, and measure 50 feet around. A typical mature sequoia weighs in at over two million pounds.

Among the many notable trees here are the Grizzly Giant, almost two millennia old and 96 feet around at its base, and the fallen Wawona Tunnel Tree, in which a hole was cut that allowed thousands of automobiles and other vehicles to pass through and be photographed before the tree toppled in 1969. There are over five hundred sequoias here in two related groves, the Upper and Lower.

You can drive to the edge of the Lower Grove, where hiking trails lead out among the trees. The road to the Mariposa Grove is oftentimes closed in winter when the snow is deep.

Ride the Open-Air Tram

If you'd rather not hike into the Mariposa Grove, buy a ticket and board an open-air tram that will carry you out among these magnificent giants on the "Big Trees Tram Tour." In 2011 the fee was $25.50 for adults, $24 for seniors, and $18 for children (children under 5 ride free). The trams cover a 5-mile loop and leave about every 20 minutes.

The first tram departs at 9 a.m., and the last tram leaves at 4 p.m. The trip takes slightly less than an hour, but you'd be well advised to get off the tram and spend a little time walking in the grove. The trams do not operate during the winter.

There are three regular stopping points along the route: the Grizzly Giant, the fallen Tunnel Tree, and the Mariposa Grove Museum. On your way back down, consider getting off at the Grizzly Giant and taking the 0.8-mile walk back to the parking lot. It's all downhill and remarkably relaxing.

Be sure to visit the Mariposa Grove Museum, where there are exhibits about the giant sequoias. Books and other literature are available for purchase. Restrooms are located there, too.

Walk in the Sequoia Forest

All trails into the Mariposa Grove of Big Trees are uphill. From the trailhead at the far end of the parking lot, there is an elevation gain of about 1,000 feet to the Upper Grove, where the fallen Wawona Tunnel Tree is located, a distance of 2.5 miles. The going is gradual, however (twenty-two children from Mrs. McDaniel's second-grade class made it up and back!), and walking is the best way to appreciate the majesty and serenity of these stately trees. Be sure to check park hiking guidelines before you take off (see page 90).

Notable Sequoias of the Mariposa Grove

Name	Diameter at Base	Height
Clothespin Tree	22 ft.	266 ft.
California Tree	23 ft.	232 ft.
Columbia Tree	28 ft.	290 ft.
General Grant Tree	29 ft.	290 ft.
Washington Tree	30 ft.	238 ft.
Grizzly Giant	31 ft	209 ft.
Lafayette Tree	31 ft.	267 ft.
Faithful Couple	40 ft.	248 ft.

Easier Hikes in the Mariposa Grove

The Grizzly Giant

From the parking lot it's only 0.8 mile and a 400-foot climb to the Grizzly Giant, one of the largest and oldest trees in the Mariposa Grove. Along the way you'll encounter lots of other sequoias and get a personal perspective on the mammoth scale of these trees. Allow from one to two hours for the round trip.

Wawona Point

This excellent lookout on the entire Wawona basin is a short walk from the top of the Mariposa Grove. Get off the tram at the fallen Wawona Tunnel Tree and walk back to the north to the Galen Clark Tree, where the old road to Wawona Point branches off. Ask your tram driver for directions if you need them. This is only a 0.5-mile walk, and you'll be able to see back to the Wawona Meadow and golf course, with views to the east of Wawona Dome. The round trip walk should take you less than an hour.

Mariposa Grove Parking Lot from the Wawona Tunnel Tree

It's always easier to hike downhill, so why not ride the tram to the top of the grove and get off at the Wawona Tunnel Tree? The hike down through the Upper and Lower Groves leads past the Mariposa Grove Museum and just about every significant sequoia in the area. It's only 2.5 miles back to your car and shouldn't require more than two to three hours to complete.

The Bachelor and Three Graces

The road to Glacier Point leaves Wawona Road at Chinquapin junction, 9 miles south of Yosemite Valley and 12 miles north of Wawona. The route winds 16 miles to the amazing promontory at Glacier Point, passing a variety of sites and attractions along the way, most of them short hikes from the road. The route is open to the point from late May through October or so, but in winter the road is plowed of snow only as far as Badger Pass, the downhill ski area 6 miles from Chinquapin. Be sure to carry tire chains in your car if you're heading out Glacier Point Road during the off-season.

Stare at the Stars

During the summer, ranger naturalists maintain a large telescope at Glacier Point and schedule regular evening programs that make use of it. There aren't many better spots for gazing at the heavens, plus you'll have the help of knowledgeable astronomers. Check the *Yosemite Guide* for dates and times and for the schedule of other ranger-led programs and hikes at Glacier Point and Bridalveil Creek Campground.

Hike, Hike, and More Hike

Given its proximity to the south rim of Yosemite Valley, Glacier Point Road provides a series of natural trailheads for spectacular day hikes. And thanks to DNC, you have the option of walking all the way down to Yosemite Valley without needing to go back and retrieve your car. During the summer, the concessioner operates a tour bus from the valley to Glacier Point. The tours run three times a day; check the bus schedule before hiking one direction. Call (209) 372-4386 or visit http://www.yosemitepark.com/Activities_ GuidedBusTours_GlacierPointTour.aspx for information.

Strap on Some Skis or a Board

Badger Pass, six miles from Chinquapin out Glacier Point Road, is the center of Yosemite ski activity during the winter. Not only are there ski lifts, ski and snowboard rentals, and a lodge, but crosscountry skiers are encouraged to utilize the groomed tracks out Glacier Point Road. (see page 22)

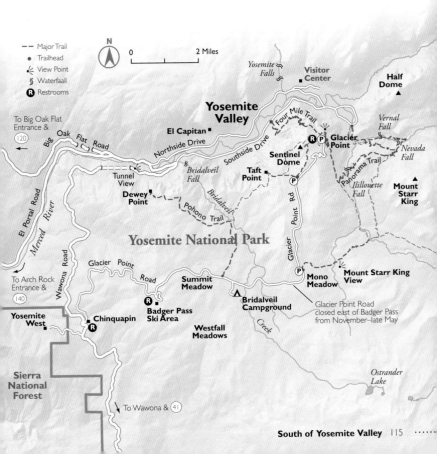

Dewey Point

This commanding viewpoint (7,385 feet) offers one of the most interesting perspectives on Bridalveil Fall and El Capitan. The trail starts 0.2 miles west of (before you get to) Bridalveil Creek Campground on Glacier Point Road (look for the sign at McGurk Meadow). There are trail markers on both sides of the road: you will want to head north. The route meanders through forest and meadows, intersects with the Pohono Trail (go left), then extends to the valley rim. Here the rock abruptly falls away, leaving you on the edge of Yosemite Valley. Be careful! While there's not much elevation gain or loss, the round trip is approximately 7 miles. Allow four to six hours for the out-and-back hike.

The view from Sentinel Dome

Mono Meadow and Mt. Starr King View

From the parking area 2.5 miles beyond Bridalveil Creek Campground on Glacier Point Road, this trail leads to the east and to a terrific spot for admiring Mt. Starr King, Half Dome, and Clouds Rest. You will drop steeply for 0.5 miles to Mono Meadow, then continue a mile farther to an unmarked clearing and the view, which you can't miss. Stop short of the switchbacks down to Illilouette Creek. The 3-mile round trip (a little strenuous on the way back) should take about three hours.

Taft Point

Unusual rock formations and an overhanging lookout point reward hikers on this short route. Start at the parking lot on Glacier Point Road about six miles past Bridalveil Creek Campground (it's on the left, when you first catch a glimpse of Sentinel Dome). The trail is mostly flat and slightly downhill to the Fissures (wide gaps in the rock hundreds of feet deep) and Taft Point, where you'll be standing on the only solid object between you and the valley floor leagues below you. Again, take care not to fall. Be thorough in your investigation of the point, which offers up several unique views. It's just over two miles round-trip; give yourself two hours.

Sentinel Dome

The trailheads for this hike and the one to Taft Point are the same. Park on the left about six miles past Bridalveil Creek Campground on Glacier Point Road (about where you first eye Sentinel Dome). The 1.1-mile hike to the top is a small price to pay for the 360 degree panorama of Yosemite's unbelievable landscape. You'll be at 8,122 feet (more than 4,000 feet above the Yosemite Valley floor); it's a good idea to have a park map for landmark identification. Try this easy hike at sunrise or sunset or on the night of a full moon (if you do, bring a good flashlight or headlamp). The round trip requires about two hours.

Yosemite Valley

Take the tour bus (see page 115) or have someone shuttle you to Glacier Point and then walk back down to Yosemite Valley over the Four-Mile Trail (4.8 miles) or via the Panorama Trail by way of Nevada and Vernal falls (8.5 miles). The Four-Mile Trail begins to the left of Glacier Point and follows a series of switchbacks down the face of the south valley wall. It terminates about a mile west of Yosemite Village on Southside Drive. The Panorama Trail begins to the right of the concession building behind the amphitheater, heading south to the top of Illilouette Fall, then back north and east to Nevada Fall. There are two routes to the valley, either the John Muir Trail or the Mist Trail (see page 93) and trail's end at Happy Isles (bus stop 16). Figure on three to four hours to hike the Four-Mile Trail and allow six to eight hours to travel the Panorama Cliffs route.

Camping South of Yosemite Valley

The campgrounds in this part of the park tend to be less busy and crowded than those in the valley, though in summer they are full every night. Advance reservations are required for the Wawona Campground between May and September, but Bridalveil Creek Campground is operated on a first-come, first-served basis when it is open between July and September. In campgrounds where no reservations are allowed, visitors will do well to arrive as early as possible to arrange for a camping spot, because check-out time is 12 noon.

Camping regulations are roughly the same as those for Yosemite Valley (see page 95). Pets are allowed in designated sites in both the Wawona and Bridalveil Creek campgrounds, and there are no showers in any park campground. The camping limit is 30 days per calendar year south of Yosemite Valley, but there is a 14-day limit at Bridalveil Creek Campground, and a 7-day limit at Wawona Campground, during summer.

Wawona Campground

This popular spot is located at the 4,000 foot elevation on the banks of the South Fork of the Merced River, approximately 25 miles south of Yosemite Valley on Wawona Road. The daily fee for the sites here is $20, and the campground is open all year (prepare for extreme cold and snow in the winter, however).

Bridalveil Creek Campground

You'll find this group of campsites 9 miles out Glacier Point Road from Chinquapin (about 25 miles from Yosemite Valley). Open from July through early September, the campground is much cooler than Yosemite Valley or Wawona, given its location at over 7,000 feet. The nightly fee is $14.

Group Campgrounds

Sections of the Wawona and Bridalveil Creek campgrounds have been set aside for use by organized groups only. Reservations can be made through Recreation.gov (see page 15); groups of between 13 and 30 people are allowed in each campsite, where only tent camping is allowed. Pets are not permitted in group sites. There are also horse camps at both the Wawona and Bridalveil Creek campgrounds. Group campsites cost $40 a night. For more information, call (209) 375-9535.

Camping in the forest

Gas

The only gas station in this part of the park is located in Wawona, just north of the Wawona Hotel on the main highway. The self-serve facility accepts major credit cards (it's a Chevron station), it's open year-round, and tire chains are available. It has a AAA rating.

For towing services, call (209) 372-8320 at any time of the day or night.

Food: Restaurants

For anything other than snacks and simple sandwiches, there's only one choice in the south end of the park—the Wawona Hotel Dining Room. Within a half-hour's drive of the South Entrance, there are a number of good restaurants along Highway 41 between Fish Camp and Oakhurst. The following places to eat are open seasonally; be sure to check the *Yosemite Guide* for dates and hours of operation.

Wawona Hotel Dining Room

Serving breakfast, lunch, and dinner from Easter week through October and on holidays in the fall and winter. Located in the Victorian main building at the hotel, the dining room has retained a historic feel. The sepia-toned photographs by Carleton Watkins and the sequoia-cone light fixtures are perfect touches in this charming, multi-windowed facility. The food is fine, the wine list good, and there's a full bar. In summer there are a few tables on the porch for outdoor dining, and they

Wawona Hotel

also serve in the bar area. There's cocktail service on the verandas and in the lobby lounge. Lunch and Sunday brunch are served buffet-style. On Saturdays in summer try the outdoor barbeque on the hotel lawn. Reservations are advised for groups of ten or more; call (209) 375-1425 for more information. Moderate to expensive.

Wawona Golf Shop Snack Stand

Open spring through fall inside the golf shop at the Wawona Hotel. Cold drinks, hot dogs, prepackaged sandwiches, and other simple items are available for those in a hurry or in need of a light meal or snack. Moderate prices.

Glacier Point Snack Stand

A summer and fall operation (10 a.m. to 5 p.m.) with a limited menu, primarily providing munchies for visitors to Glacier Point. Moderate prices.

Food: Groceries

Campers, vacation home renters, and park visitors have the following two choices for groceries in the park south of Yosemite Valley. Check the *Yosemite Guide* for operating hours, or call the indicated numbers.

Wawona Grocery Store

Located adjacent to the gas station just off the main highway and north of the Wawona Hotel. Phone (209) 375-6574.

The Pine Tree Market

You'll find this store in the heart of the community of North Wawona. It's less than a mile east of the main highway on Chilnualna Falls Road. Phone (209) 375-6343.

Lodging

Wawona is the only area in the park where the majority of lodgings are not operated by DNC, the park's main concessioner. The Wawona Hotel is part of the DNC system, and to reserve a room there, you should follow the steps which are detailed on page 14. You must contact each of the other lodging providers directly to reserve from them.

Wawona Hotel

Open from Easter week through October and on weekends and holidays through Christmas. This is the oldest resort hotel in California; the structure to the right of the main hotel building was built in 1879. The whitewashing, wide porches, well-kept grounds, and an old-fashioned bathing tank (we call them swimming pools now) all suggest another era in Yosemite's history. It's a remarkably peaceful and relaxing setting, but guests should keep in mind that some of the rooms are one hundred years old. Rooms with a private bath rent for a bit more than those that share a community bathroom.

Besides the dining room, the Wawona Hotel incorporates a golf course with pro shop and snack bar, tennis courts, and a cocktail lounge. Be sure to listen for beloved piano man Tom Bopp, who performs nightly in the lobby.

The Redwoods Guest Cottages

Open year-round. This is a collection of about 130 privately owned vacation homes and cabins available for rental on a daily or weekly basis. Located in the privately held section of Wawona near the South Fork of the Merced (approximately 1 mile out Chilnualna Falls Road), the rentals vary in size from 1 to 6 bedrooms and all have kitchens and fireplaces. Rates vary with the seasons and range from $143 to $643 plus tax per night; there is a two-night minimum. For information call (888) 225-6666, write to P.O. Box 2085, Wawona, CA 95389, or visit the website at www.redwoodsinyosemite.com.

Yosemite's Scenic Wonders Vacation Rentals

Open year-round. Located in Yosemite West, just beyond the park boundary, but accessible only via park roads, these rental units are situated about halfway between Yosemite Valley and Wawona. Their proximity (8 miles) to the Badger Pass ski area has made the condos a favorite of winter visitors. But cool summer temperatures and the short drive to Yosemite Valley (about half an hour) make Yosemite West popular at other times of year as well. At 6,000 feet above sea level, this area has snow into the sunny days of late spring, and you can have a snowball fight in a t-shirt. Rates vary depending on unit size and the season. Information can be had by calling (888) 967-3648, a toll-free number, or www.scenicwonders.com. Moderate to expensive.

Yosemite West Lodging

Open year-round. This company handles the rental of a collection of studios, apartments, townhouses, duplexes, individual cottages, vacation homes, and mountain homes in the Yosemite West development. These are located just west of the park, less than one mile south of Chinquapin off the Wawona Road (15 miles from Yosemite Valley and 8 miles from Badger Pass). All units have televisions and kitchens. Rates range quite a bit and discounts are available for longer stays. For reservations and information call (559) 642-2211, or write P.O. Box 2325, Oakhurst, CA 93644-2325. The website is at www.yosemitewest.com. Moderate to expensive.

Wawona Golf Course

Tuolumne Meadows

6 | North of Yosemite Valley

Over two-thirds of Yosemite National Park lies north of Yosemite Valley, much of that region being wilderness. The area is made accessible primarily by Tioga Road, the only trans-Sierra crossing between Walker Pass, in Kern County, and Sonora Pass, to the north. Spectacular high-country terrain, brilliant blue lakes, and astounding granite peaks are reached via this route that leads through Tuolumne Meadows, the largest subalpine meadows in the Sierra Nevada. The road crests the range at 9,945-foot Tioga Pass.

Map of Hetch Hetchy, Tioga Road,

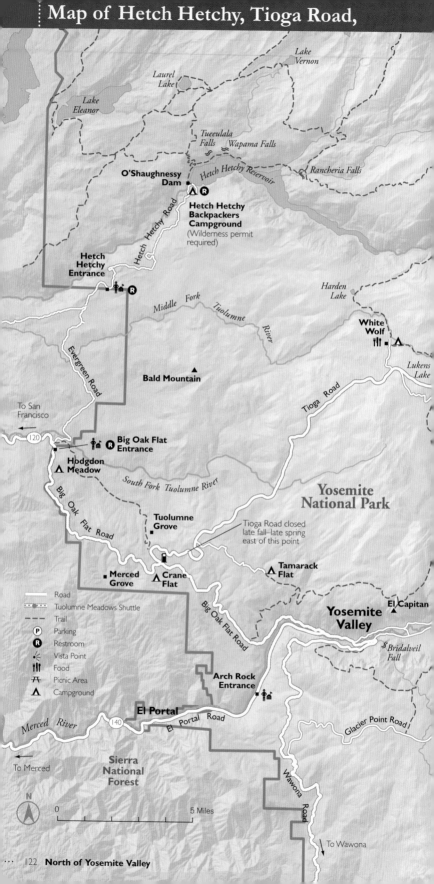

Lake Vernon

Laurel Lake

Lake Eleanor

Tueeulala Falls   Wapama Falls

Rancheria Falls

O'Shaughnessy Dam

Hetch Hetchy Reservoir

Hetch Hetchy Backpackers Campground
(Wilderness permit required)

Hetch Hetchy Entrance

Hetch Hetchy Road

Middle   Fork   Tuolumne   River

Harden Lake

White Wolf

Lukens Lake

Evergreen Road

Bald Mountain

Tioga Road

To San Francisco

←

120

Big Oak Flat Entrance

Hodgdon Meadow

South Fork Tuolumne River

Yosemite National Park

Big Oak Flat Road

Tuolumne Grove

Tioga Road closed late fall–late spring east of this point

Merced Grove

Crane Flat

Tamarack Flat

El Capitan

Yosemite Valley

Big Oak Flat Road

Bridalveil Fall

Legend

—— Road
······ Tuolumne Meadows Shuttle
- - - Trail
P Parking
R Restroom
⚞ Vista Point
⚏ Food
☰ Picnic Area
△ Campground

Arch Rock Entrance

El Portal

140

El Portal Road

Glacier Point Road

Merced River

← To Merced

Sierra National Forest

Wawona Road

N

0   5 Miles

To Wawona

McCabe Lakes

Roosevelt Lake

▲ Mount Conness

th Fork Tuolumne River

Young Lakes

Glen Aulin ⛺ High Sierra Camp

Ten Lakes

Tuolumne Meadows

To Tioga Pass Entrance & Lee Vining via (120)

Lembert Dome ▲

Grant Lakes

Yosemite Creek

May Lake

Ⓡ Ⓟ Ⓐ ▲

Ⓡ Ⓟ

Mt Hoffman ▲

Ⓡ 🚻 🏛 🏪 🛖 Ⓡ

Visitor Center

Tuolumne Meadows Campground

May Lake ⛺ High Sierra Camp

Ⓡ 🥾

Ⓡ

Cathedral ▲ Peak

Elizabeth Lake

Ⓡ 🥾

Ⓡ

Yosemite Creek

Tenaya Lake

Facilities along Tioga Road available summer only

Porcupine Flat 🥾

Ⓡ

Olmsted Point

Evelyn Lake

⛺ Sunrise High Sierra Camp

Vogelsang ⛺ High Sierra Camp

Clouds Rest ▲

North Dome 🥾 ▲

Bernice Lake

semite lls

Valley Visitor Center

Merced River

Merced Lake

Half Dome ▲

Vernal Fall

Washburn Lake

Glacier Point

Nevada Fall

▲ Mt Clark

Ostrander Lake

Illilouette Creek

Edna Lake

Ottoway Lakes

Sierra National Forest

Tenaya Lake

The Summit of Mount Hoffmann

This is the geographic center of Yosemite, with extraordinary views in every direction. See page 131.

The Beach at Tenaya Lake

Unbelievably fine on a warm day, a terrific spot anytime. Enjoy a picnic or a swim, or simply take a nap. See page 128.

The Turnout at Olmsted Point

To see the vast expanse of glacier-carved granite is worth the stop alone. But there's much more—and marmots, too. See page 129.

The Hike to the Merced Grove

Easy and quiet. Plus this is Yosemite's most remote and least-visited sequoia grove. See page 126.

A Meal on the Porch of White Wolf Lodge

Lunch and dinner are likely times to sit outside at this quaint spot and watch the White Wolf meadow do whatever meadows do. See page 140.

A Visit to Hetch Hetchy Reservoir

This body of water occupies a valley which has been characterized as Yosemite Valley's little brother. It has retained much of its beauty and offers great hiking. See page 125.

The Trail into Lyell Canyon

The Lyell Fork of the Tuolumne River is one of the park's most peaceful and inspiring settings. The trail leads to and along its course. See page 137.

The High Sierra Camps

Whether you hike the full loop or visit just one of these five backcountry encampments, the experience will be unique. Stop for a mind-blowing meal, or pamper yourself by staying over. See page 132.

White Cascade, Glen Aulin High Sierra Camp

The Hetch Hetchy area of Yosemite, as it is called in this book, includes the portion of the park that is found on its western boundary along Big Oak Flat Road north of Crane Flat, and along Evergreen and Hetch Hetchy roads (see page 127). The region is best known for its two groves of giant sequoias (the Merced and Tuolumne Groves) and for the Hetch Hetchy Reservoir on the Tuolumne River.

National Park Service offices here are located at the Big Oak Flat Entrance, where there are a ranger station (209-379-1899), a campground reservation office, a small visitor center and book sales area, a wilderness permit and reservation office, and public restrooms. If you've entered the park from the west over Highway 120, this is a good place to orient yourself; Yosemite Valley is still 25 miles away. There's also an entrance station at Mather, about eight miles from the Big Oak Flat Entrance on the way to Hetch Hetchy. This road is open during daylight hours only and sometimes closes for snow. Call (209) 372-0200 to check on it.

The route to Hetch Hetchy Reservoir is over Evergreen Road, located just north of the park off Highway 120. If traveling from the south, leave the park through the Big Oak Flat Entrance. The right turn onto Evergreen Road is one mile past the entrance station. From the north, turn left on Evergreen Road one mile before you reach the park on Highway 120. Hetch Hetchy is 16 miles out this road, which becomes Hetch Hetchy Road at Camp Mather (bear right at the intersection).

Hetch Hetchy: The Dam

Many wonder how a feature like Hetch Hetchy Reservoir came to be sited within the boundaries of a national park. It wasn't easy or quick, but when the political struggle ended, the scenic qualities of Hetch Hetchy Valley had been "submerged" for the good of the citizens of San Francisco and their thirsts.

The city had been looking for a dependable supply of mountain water when, shortly after the turn of the century, Hetch Hetchy was proposed as the perfect location for a dam site. The notion of a reservoir in Yosemite was not universally attractive, however, and John Muir, the Sierra Club, and others opposed the project and fought it for many years. On several occasions the Hetch Hetchy project was

outright rejected. But the city fathers were persistent, and in 1913 the Raker Bill granting San Francisco permission to dam the Tuolumne River at Hetch Hetchy was passed in Congress.

Losing the fight to save Hetch Hetchy devastated Muir. Many believe that his efforts left him exhausted and contributed greatly to his death about a year later. On the other hand, the reservoir proved an enormous success for the city of San Francisco. Much of the Bay Area still relies on the project for the bulk of its water and power.

The dam was constructed beginning in 1919 and took about four years to finish. The resulting reservoir is eight miles long, has a capacity of over 117 million gallons, and covers 1,861 surface acres (three square miles). The dam itself is 410 feet high, 910 feet long, and 308 feet thick at its base, which tapers to 24 feet at the top. One interesting fact about the Hetch Hetchy project is that the water in the system pipelines flows all the way to San Francisco by gravity!

O'Shaughnessy Dam in Hetch Hetchy Valley

The Hetch Hetchy area is best enjoyed in spring and fall. Hetch Hetchy Reservoir's setting is more foothill than montane, and gray pines, manzanita, and lower-elevation wildflowers are abundant there. The area's other attractions are much higher, averaging about 6,000 feet above sea level. These higher elevations feature sugar pines, sequoias, and the most accessible winter hiking in Yosemite. Stop at the Big Oak Flat Information Station (at the park entrance) to get oriented.

Hetch Hetchy Reservoir

Walk through the Merced Grove

Yosemite's quietest stand of sequoias is the Merced Grove, accessible only on foot. It's a two-mile hike into the grove from the trailhead on Big Oak Flat Road. Located 3.5 miles north of Crane Flat, or 4.5 miles south of the Big Oak Flat Entrance, the trailhead is marked by road signs.

Follow the dirt road for about a mile, then take the left fork down into the grove. This is the park's smallest group of sequoias (about twenty trees), probably first discovered in 1833 by the Joseph R. Walker party. Look for the old Merced Grove cabin that was built as a ranger/entrance station but is no longer used for that purpose.

These sequoias convey the silent majesty that has characterized them for thousands of years. The absence of motorized vehicles and the solitude are a real treat for hikers to the Merced Grove. Allow three hours for the 4-mile round trip.

Hike the Tuolumne Grove

The former route of Big Oak Flat Road leads downhill from Crane Flat into the Tuolumne Grove of Big Trees, a cluster of about forty-five sequoias. This dirt road, which was open to traffic until 1993, drops steeply for about a mile to where the first big trees can be spotted. An interesting attraction in the grove is the "Dead Giant" tree, a lifeless but still standing partial tree that has been driven through by thousands of wagons and automobiles since it was tunneled out in 1878 (but no longer). There's also a self-guiding nature trail in the grove, a half-mile in length, that should take about thirty minutes to walk. If you have children with you (or even if you don't), check out Dead Fred, a hollow fallen sequoia. Starting at the roots, you can crawl through the trunk for about a hundred feet. It's a tight squeeze at the end, but there's an outlet halfway down.

The trail to the Tuolumne Grove takes off near Crane Flat. From the intersection of Big Oak Flat Road and Tioga Road, take Tioga Road one mile to the east (towards Tuolumne Meadows). Turn left into the Tuolumne Grove parking lot. The route is obvious; the round trip of about two miles is relatively easy, though it's all uphill on the way back.

Let Them Entertain You

In summer, National Park Service rangers conduct a variety of walks, programs, and campfires. Activities are centered at Crane Flat Campground and in the Tuolumne Grove, though other locales are used from time to time. Check the *Yosemite Guide* under White Wolf/Crane Flat/Big Oak Flat Visitor Activities for details and times.

Lookout for Fire

The Crane Flat Fire Lookout is staffed during the summer, when the National Park Service watches the surrounding forests for signs of smoke. Visitors are welcome at the facility, which can be reached over a primitive road leading off to the east less than one mile north of Crane Flat on Big Oak Flat Road. It's a 0.5-mile uphill trip to the lookout.

Watch for fire and other emergency vehicles along the way. The view from the lookout is a special one with glimpses of the park in every direction. It's also fun to cross-country ski here in winter.

Hike Hetch Hetchy

Though the once beautiful valley of Hetch Hetchy might be lost forever, many of its scenic wonders can still be appreciated. Tueeulala and Wapama falls still thunder from the north rim, Kolana

Rock rises imposingly from the reservoir's southern shore, and a remarkable variety of plant and animal life populates the perimeter.

While Hetch Hetchy is at roughly the same elevation as Yosemite Valley, it's much warmer. In the middle of summer it's downright hot. Perfect months for day hiking are October through May. You'd be amazed at how warm the north side of the reservoir can be in the dead of winter. The main trail at Hetch Hetchy leads over the dam, through a tunnel, and along the north edge. The undulating route passes Tueeulala Falls, Wapama Falls (about two miles from the dam), and Rancheria Falls (six and a half miles out). Hike as far or as little as you like. In spring, be prepared at Wapama Falls for the high water and heavy mist that sometimes force closure of the trail. Retrace your steps back to the dam.

Fishing is allowed in Hetch Hetchy Reservoir, but swimming and boating are not.

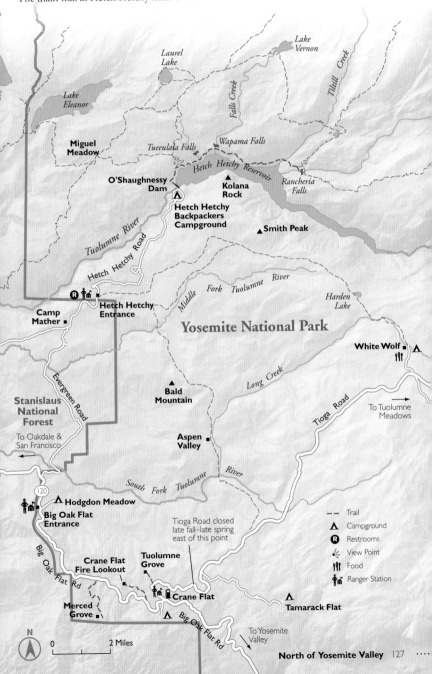

Originally a wagon road across Tioga Pass built by the Great Consolidated Silver Company in 1883, Tioga Road literally splits Yosemite National Park in two. Improved to its present condition and alignment in 1961, the road opened up some of Yosemite's most stunning country and allowed access to previously remote high-country destinations. Today the Tioga Road corridor is rife with scenic and recreational opportunities.

Gaylor Lakes

For the purposes of this book, Tioga Road refers to the area of the park along Tioga Road (which extends from Crane Flat to Tioga Pass, some 46 miles east) except for the Tuolumne Meadows area.

Visitors should be aware that Tioga Road is not open all year. Heavy snows require the National Park Service to close the road (from November until May or June, usually), though snow is a possibility in any season. Typically mild summer weather attracts both recreationists and travelers headed east in large numbers. There are plenty of options for fun along the road, with multiple campgrounds, trailheads, lakes, streams, and scenic views to choose from. For information

and assistance, there is a ranger station at the Tioga Pass Entrance (as well as the Tuolumne Meadows Visitor Center, described on page 133).

Whether you're just passing through or making a leisurely trip along Tioga Road, your experience will be a better one if you know where you are and what you're seeing. A valuable aid in this regard is the *Yosemite Road Guide*. It's available at stores throughout the park or from the Yosemite Conservancy. How else will you know about "Smoky Jack," the old Tioga Road, Siesta Lake, and the ghost forest?

Get in over Your Head

The best place to have a swim along Tioga Road is Tenaya Lake. The park's largest lake, it is located approximately 8 miles west of Tuolumne Meadows, or 30 miles east of Crane Flat. The inviting sandy beach on the eastern shore is a good bet, but be prepared for some cold water. Use the dressing rooms and bathrooms in the parking lot just east of the lake. If it's too cold to swim, have a picnic in this dramatic setting. If you're at Tenaya Lake in late summer, check out the tree trunks rising from the water—long ago there was a forest here, and the icy, oxygen-poor water preserves the trees to this day.

Be Programmed

During summer, ranger naturalists offer free programs for visitors at various locations along Tioga Road. Check the *Yosemite Guide* for details.

Hike All You Like

The territory stretching out to the north and south of Tioga Road is a veritable hiker's wonderland. From numerous points along the route, trails lead into a landscape unequalled anywhere in the world. Hikes range from easy to very strenuous, becoming more difficult with increased elevation. Follow basic hiking precautions (see page 90), and in this high-country setting, stay hydrated by drinking lots of liquids. The most common hiking-related ailment is altitude sickness; consider spending a day or so getting acclimatized before starting to hike.

For those hikers who travel to Yosemite without a car or who wish to leave their vehicles in Yosemite Valley, DNC operates a hikers' bus that traverses the length of Tioga Road each day from approximately July 1 to Labor Day. You can arrange to

The view from Olmsted Point

get off at trailheads along the way. The bus returns to Yosemite Valley every afternoon. For information, call (209) 372-4386 or visit http://www.yosemitepark.com/activities_ guidedbustours_tuolumnemeadows.aspx. YARTS also provides service along Tioga Road. For information, call (877) 989-2787 or visit http://www.yarts.com/.

Wet a Line

Fishing can be amazingly good along Tioga Road. Spots like Lukens Lake, Harden Lake, Tenaya Lake, and May Lake (all described in this chapter) are home to many feisty, if somewhat small, trout. Yosemite Creek and the Dana Fork of the Tuolumne River can also yield up a fish or two. The general park fishing regulations apply (see page 89); check with a park ranger for any special rules.

Check Out Half Dome's Back Side

One of Yosemite's most remarkable scenic overlooks is found at Olmsted Point, and it shouldn't be missed. This major pullout is located 2.5 miles west of Tenaya Lake and just slightly more than 2 miles east of the May Lake turnoff. Here the grandeur of the granite walls of Tenaya Canyon is revealed. Beyond loom the less-seen northern and eastern faces of Half Dome and Clouds Rest. To the east, the landscape includes Tenaya Lake and the

many domes and peaks of the Tuolumne Meadows region. A short nature trail leads down from the point, and watch for fat and sassy marmots in the rocks (but please don't feed them).

Harden Lake

This is a relatively flat 3-mile walk to an attractive little lake that offers picnicking, swimming, and fishing. Start in front of the White Wolf Campground and head north on what was the original Tioga Road. You can follow the road all the way to the lake or catch a trail branching off about a mile from it. If you take the road, bear to the right when it forks. There's a good view of the Tuolumne River Canyon from the far side of the lake. The round trip is about 6 miles and should take about four hours.

Lukens Lake

It's somewhat uphill, but this hike of less than a mile terminates at a lovely spot amid meadow flowers and grasses. Being so close to the road, Lukens Lake is perfect for families with young (but not infant) children. Take your fishing poles and a picnic lunch. The trailhead is found 1.8 miles to the east of the White Wolf intersection, or 3 miles west of the spot where Tioga Road crosses Yosemite Creek. Head north up the hill, then drop down to the lake. This easy hike is not quite 2 miles up and back and requires about an hour to cover (a little longer for families!). You can also reach Lukens Lake from White Wolf. Ask for trail directions at the lodge.

Yosemite Creek to the Valley

From the point on Tioga Road where it crosses Yosemite Creek (about 5 miles east of the White Wolf turnoff), a trail leads southward over level and downhill terrain all the way to Yosemite Valley. Because it's a one-way hike of 13 miles, you'll have to arrange for a ride to the trailhead, plan on shuttling back to pick up your car on Tioga Road, or use the hikers' bus mentioned on page 129. The trail follows Yosemite Creek down to Yosemite Creek Campground and eventually to the top of Yosemite Falls. Check out the spectacular view from the top (see page 93) before descending the final 3.5 miles to the Yosemite Valley floor. This is a hike for the physically fit, demanding but satisfying. Allow at least eight hours.

North Dome

This difficult hike to one of the best views of Yosemite Valley (see page 100) takes off to the south of Tioga Road, about 5 miles beyond the point where the road crosses Yosemite Creek (this is also 2 miles west of the May Lake turnoff and just east of Porcupine Flat Campground). The walk is mostly downhill and flat for 4.2 miles to the dome. Watch for the erratic boulders left by the glaciers here, and check out the impressive view of Half Dome directly across from you. Because the return trip to Tioga Road is mostly uphill, this should be considered a strenuous hike. Give yourself six to eight hours for the 8.5-mile trip out and back.

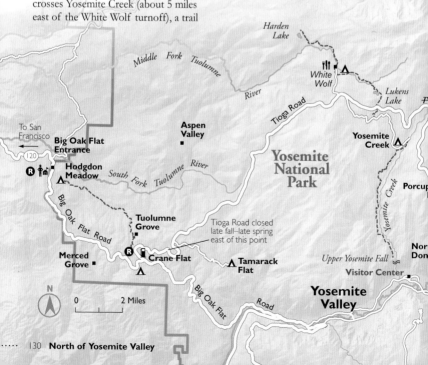

May Lake and Mt. Hoffmann

Great for those who like to get in the middle of things, Mt. Hoffmann is the geographic center of Yosemite National Park. It offers superb views of the park's high country from its 10,850-foot summit. The route up the mountain leads past idyllic May Lake, the location of one of the High Sierra Camps (see page 132). Start your hike at the May Lake parking area. Turn north off Tioga Road about 5 miles west of Tenaya Lake and drive 2 miles to the parking lot. It's an easy 1.25 miles to May Lake, and the 2 miles beyond to the top of Mt. Hoffmann are much more strenuous but worth the effort (you will gain about 1,500 feet in elevation). Plan on two hours round trip for May Lake, and add three to four more for the ascent of Mt. Hoffmann.

Mono Pass

This high elevation hike is a comparatively easy 4 miles with an elevation gain of only 1,000 feet. The route, however, begins at nearly 10,000 feet and almost reaches the 11,000-foot level (prepare for some heavy breathing). The trail begins 1.5 miles west of Tioga Pass and heads south along an old Indian trading route. At Mono Pass are the remains of several mining buildings and cabins from the late 1800s. Views of Mt. Gibbs and Mt. Dana are extremely fine. This 8-mile round trip takes from four to six hours depending upon your fitness level.

Gaylor Lakes

Here's another trip for high-elevation freaks who love to huff and puff. The trail ascends steeply to the north from just a few feet west of the Tioga Pass Entrance Station, which is 9,945 feet high. Middle Gaylor Lake is about a mile from the trailhead, but it's no easy climb. Follow the inflowing creek to Upper Gaylor Lake and the remnants of a stone shelter at the Great Sierra Mine 300 yards to its north. This is truly an alpine environment, with few trees, strong winds, and often harsh weather. Allow three hours for this moderately difficult hike of 4 miles round trip.

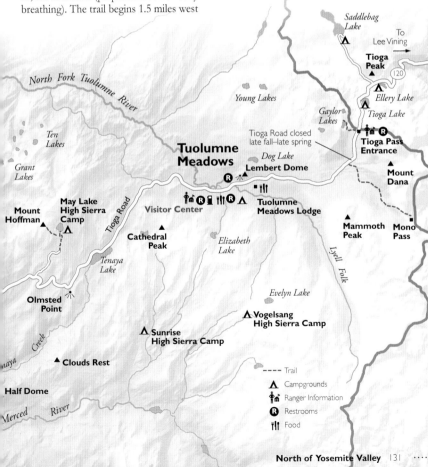

The High Sierra Camps

Five rustic colonies of tents in the park's loftier regions constitute an institution unique to Yosemite called the High Sierra Camps. Placed in a roughly circular pattern about one day's hike apart, the camps allow visitors to enjoy high-elevation backcountry in semi-luxury, with wholesome hot meals prepared by the camp staff, and regulation beds with mattresses, pillows, woolen blankets, and comforters that await weary travelers. There are even showers!

The idea for the camps originated with Washington B. Lewis, Yosemite's first NPS superintendent. He wanted hikers to enjoy Yosemite's high country free from the "irksome" load normally needed for a backcountry trip. In 1924 the first camps were installed at a number of locations (several already were unofficial "High Sierra camps"), and the system was underway.

Over the years there have been as many as eight different camps, including Little Yosemite Valley, Boothe Lake, Lyell Canyon, and Tenaya Lake, but the present configuration has been set for quite some time. The camps are open for a very short season (roughly late June or early July to Labor Day) and are operated by DNC Parks & Resorts at Yosemite.

Many people use Tuolumne Lodge (see page 141) as a starting or ending point for the High Sierra Loop Trip. In a clockwise direction from Tuolumne Meadows the other camps are Vogelsang, Merced Lake,

Sunrise, May Lake, and Glen Aulin. The distance from one to the next averages nine miles. Guests at the High Sierra Camps are accommodated in dormitory-style tents that sleep either four or six. The communal bathhouses offer running water, showers, and toilets. Guests must provide their own sheets or sleep-sacks and towels. Hearty breakfasts and dinners are served daily, and bag lunches can be ordered. Sizes of the camps vary, but about 35 people on average can be lodged.

A favorite of many High Sierra Camp users is the 7-day guided loop trip (there's also a 5-day option). A naturalist accompanies a maximum of 14 people, providing ongoing interpretation of the geology and natural history of Yosemite's wilderness. There are campfire programs nightly, and members of the group develop a real spirit of camaraderie and friendship.

Despite the price (at least $145 plus tax per night), the camps are fully booked almost every night of the summer. Reservations are essential and are handled by lottery. Applications are accepted each year between September 1 and November 1 for the lottery and applicants are notified of the results by mid-January. For information: http://www.yosemitepark.com/accommodations.aspx. For an application: High Sierra Desk, Yosemite Reservations, 6771 North Palm Ave., Fresno, CA 93704.

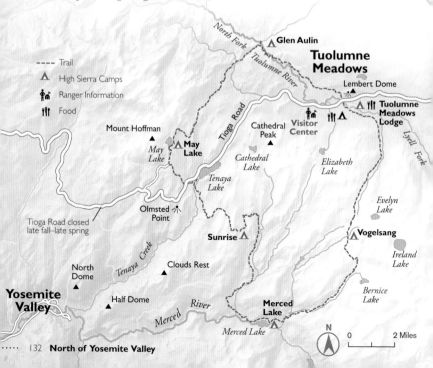

Map labels:

To Glen Aulin 5.3 mi

To Young Lakes 6.5 mi

To Young Lakes 6.5 mi

N

0 | 1 Mile

North Fork Tuolumne River

Dog Lake

Tioga Road closed late fall–late spring

Pothole Dome ▲

To Yosemite Valley 56 mi

Campground Reservations Office

Lembert Dome ▲

To Tioga Pass & (120) 7 mi

Tuolumne Meadows

Tioga Road

Store/Grill

Wilderness Permits

Tuolumne Meadows Lodge

Fairview Dome ▲

Visitor Center

Tuolumne Meadows Campground

To Cathedral Lakes 3.5 mi and Sunrise 7.8 mi

Budd Creek

Unicorn Creek

Cathedral Peak ▲

Elizabeth Lake

Legend:

— Road

Shuttle Bus Route (summer-only)

- - - Trail

P Parking

R Restroom

Vista Point

Food

▲ Campground

D Dump Station

This stunningly picturesque region sits 8,600 feet up in the transparent sky of Yosemite's high country. Contained in a basin about 2.5 miles long, the meadow system may be the largest in the Sierra Nevada at the subalpine level. Tuolumne Meadows is only 55 miles by road from Yosemite Valley, but it's a world apart.

Called by some the "hub" or "heart" of the high country, Tuolumne is a seasonal phenomenon. It is closed by snow to visitation during the bulk of year, but when summer comes, the action is impressive. Hikers flock here, both day trippers and backpackers. Rock climbers who winter in Yosemite Valley adopt Tuolumne as a summer home. And visitors arrive in cars to revel in the awesome beauty of the place, and to enjoy a less-developed part of the park.

There's plenty to gawk at, too. The Tuolumne River winds its way sinuously through the meadows, while an array of unusually shaped domes rings the area. There are smooth-bottomed canyons and jagged peaks; delicate lakes and odorous springs. These multiple elements combine to create a landscape both wonderful and inspiring.

During the summer months there's a wilderness center at Tuolumne Meadows operated by the National Park Service, along with a small visitor center. The wilderness center is just off Tioga Road along the way to Tuolumne Lodge, and the visitor center is located near the halfway point of the meadows about a quarter-mile west of the gas station and store. For information or assistance call (209) 372-0263.

Tuolumne Meadows

Climb a Dome

Scrambling to the top of one of Tuolumne's granite domes can be fun and exhilarating. It can also be hazardous to your health. Try one of the easier rocks, like Lembert Dome (see page 137) or Pothole Dome (adjacent to the road at the west end of the meadows). Wear proper footgear and don't go up anything you aren't sure you can get down. Climbing lessons are available from the Mountaineering School in Tuolumne Meadows. Call (209) 372-8435 or visit http://www.yosemitepark.com/Activities_RockClimbing.aspx for details and rates.

Hikers on Lembert Dome

Take a Swim

Because they are fed by the melting snow nearby, most of the streams, rivers, and lakes of the Tuolumne region are freezing cold. As the summer progresses they warm a bit, but swimming is not for the weak of heart. There are plenty of good swimming holes along the Tuolumne River as it passes the campground, and on its fork that winds lazily through Lyell Canyon (see hiking section below). Lake swimmers should try Tenaya Lake, 7 miles to the west, Elizabeth Lake, or Dog Lake (see pages 136 and 137).

Become a Sheepwatcher

In 1986, a small herd of California bighorn sheep was transplanted to the park in the Tioga Pass region. The sheep are native to the park but were eliminated here by disease and hunting before 1900. The introduced herd leads a precarious existence (the sheep are particularly vulnerable to mountain lion predation), but it is still considered viable. Your best bet for bighorns is along the Sierra Crest, at Mono Pass or Parker Pass. Check at the visitor center for information and directions.

Get Tall in the Saddle

Riding horses are stabled at Tuolumne Meadows by DNC Parks and Resorts at Yosemite each summer. As is the case throughout the park, they offer two-hour, half-day, and all-day guided horseback trips. The Tuolumne stables can be found by turning south onto the road for Tuolumne Lodge and Tuolumne Meadows Wilderness Center, about a quarter mile east of the bridge over the Tuolumne River. For more information and rates call (209) 372-8427 or visit http://www.yosemitepark.com/Activities_MuleHorsebackRides.aspx.

Walk a Mile in Your Shoes

The hiking around Tuolumne Meadows is first-rate. The trails are varied, the scenery is exceptional, and the weather usually cooperative (but plan for afternoon thunder showers, particularly in August). A person staying at Tuolumne could take a different hike every day for a week and still not exhaust the possibilities. Be sure to follow normal hiking precautions (see page 90) and drink extra water to keep yourself hydrated at this high elevation.

A free shuttle bus runs between Tuolumne Meadows and Olmsted Point, providing service to several stops along the way, from approximately June through mid-September. It's a good way to get to your trailhead and leave your car behind. Hours are posted on signs at bus stops throughout the Tuolumne area. The DNC bus and the YARTS bus both visit Tuolumne

Dog Lake

Meadows from Yosemite Valley once a day from July 1 through Labor Day. You can be dropped off at the trailhead of your choice and, if the timing works out, be picked up later. Call (209) 372-4386 (DNC) or (877) 989-2787 (YARTS) for information, or visit http://www.yarts.com/.

Get Centered

To learn more about the Tuolumne Meadows region, visit the visitor center located south of Tioga Road a short way west of the gas station. There you'll find exhibits, knowledgeable rangers, and books and maps for sale. It's also a good place to find out about free ranger walks and programs that will be happening during your visit (or check *Yosemite Guide*).

Children can participate in the Junior Ranger program by purchasing a copy of the *Junior Ranger Handbook* (ages 3–6) or the *Little Cub Handbook* (ages 7–13) at the center. By completing the activities outlined in the handbook, they can earn certificates and badges while they learn lots more about the park. The handbooks are available at all park visitor centers; in Tuolumne call (209) 372-0263.

Do Something Fishy

Tuolumne Meadows is loaded with family fishing opportunities. These high-country trout seem to be plentiful, but they're small. Your kids will find the many rivers and lakes great places to practice their angling techniques. The Tuolumne River and its tributaries are excellent spots. You can also try Dog Lake, Cathedral Lake, and Elizabeth Lake. Follow park fishing regulations (see page 89) and check at the visitor center for information or tips.

. . . .

Q: How should a hiker behave in a lightning storm?

A: Stay clear of open expanses of water, keep off open areas of rock and out of meadows, and stay away from prominent landmarks like lone, isolated trees. Seek shelter from the storm; a dense stand of trees of roughly the same height works well.

Cathedral Lake at sunset

Cathedral Lakes

Taking off from the obvious parking area at the west end of Tuolumne Meadows (south of the road), this trail is fairly strenuous, gaining about 1,000 feet in under 4 miles. The route is uphill, then relatively flat for a while, then uphill again before it drops into the Cathedral Lakes basin. Take the right fork in the trail to reach the lower lake, which is the larger of the two. Have a swim, enjoy your lunch, or fish a little. Your view of Cathedral Peak will be outstanding. The round-trip hike is less than 8 miles and should take four to six hours.

Elizabeth Lake

It's steep and short and well worth the effort. Elizabeth Lake is a lovely spot nestled against the base of Unicorn Peak, one of Tuolumne's most recognizable landmarks. The 2.3-mile hike begins at the back side of the Tuolumne Meadows Campground (across from the bathrooms

for the group camp area), and it is just about all uphill. Given the elevation (you climb to about 9,500 feet), it's a good idea to take your time and adopt a slow but steady pace. The water's cold though swimmable, and fishing is fair. Allow from three to four hours for the 4.6-mile round trip.

Soda Springs

Here's an easy hike that's flat and perfect for all ages. The trail leads out into the middle of Tuolumne Meadows and to a naturally carbonated mineral spring that bubbles mysteriously to the surface. Park in the parking lot just north of Tioga Road, adjacent to Lembert Dome (just east of the bridge over the Tuolumne River). Follow the gravel road to the north, and where the road turns right, walk around the brown metal gate and continue north. (If you get to the stables, you're off-route.) Besides the Soda Springs, you'll find Parsons Memorial Lodge (erected in 1914 by the Sierra Club) and the McCauley Cabin, a pioneer structure now used as a ranger residence. You'll be close to the river and will get a sense of the size and beauty of the meadows. You can make the 1.5-mile walk in an hour.

Glen Aulin

To reach this aspen-studded hollow along the Tuolumne River, walk to Soda Springs (see above for hike information). The trail continues past the springs and roughly follows the river 7 miles to a small campground and one of the High Sierra Camps (see page 132). The trail is slightly downhill all the way, and that

Soda Springs

makes the hike back a stiff one. Watch for Tuolumne Falls and White Cascade as you hike. If you are truly a glutton for hiking punishment, Waterwheel Falls, one of the park's most unusual cascades, is 3.3 miles past Glen Aulin. The trip to Glen Aulin is a very strenuous hike of 14 miles round trip; give yourself eight to ten hours to accomplish it. Don't pay strict attention to the mileages on the signs—they can be contradictory and misleading.

Dog Lake

This easily reached spot is perfect for swimming, but perhaps not for fishing (there is a rumor that no fish remain within it). Follow the directions for the Lembert Dome trailhead. Once you've found the trailhead, the most challenging part of the hike is over! The trail is steep at first, then levels off for a final gradual ascent to the lake. A moderate hike of 3 miles round trip; allow four hours.

Early morning rainbow at the White Cascade

Lembert Dome

From the top of this oddly shaped dome, the 360 degree panorama of Tuolumne Meadows is fantastic. At the east end of Tuolumne Meadows turn onto the road that leads to Tuolumne Lodge. Past the ranger station but before the lodge is a parking lot on the left side of the road. Park there, walk up the bank to the north, carefully cross the main road, and begin your hike up the hill. After some steep switchbacks, the spur trail to the summit of Lembert Dome heads left. Emerge from the trees and walk the (usually) sunny, windswept granite to the top of the dome. Take your topo map for identification of the many peaks and mountains around you. There is also a nature trail from the parking lot at the base of the dome itself, but this is relatively difficult to find and follow. Up and back is about 3 miles and should require three hours of your time.

Lyell Canyon

This hike is the proverbial stroll in the park. The trail follows the Lyell Fork of the Tuolumne River out through the beautiful canyon that shares its name. The trailhead is at the west end of the parking lot for Tuolumne Lodge, but park your car in the lot for the Dog Lake hike. Head into the forest, cross a bridge, then continue to double bridges over the Lyell Fork (less than a half-mile out). You leave the river at this point and follow the trail, which rejoins the river farther out the canyon. It's a flat hike the entire route and as scenic and relaxing as they come. Lyell Canyon is about 8 miles long and you can hike as little or as much as you like. Give yourself enough time to make it back before dark.

The campgrounds at the north end of the park can be characterized as more primitive and remote and generally smaller (with Tuolumne Meadows Campground being the main exception). Only a few are handled by Recreation.gov; the balance are operated on a first-come, first-served basis. For campgrounds that can't be reserved in advance, remember that the check-out time is noon; this is the perfect hour to attempt to secure a site (although it doesn't hurt to arrive earlier, especially on weekends).

Pets are not allowed in some campgrounds, or on any of the trails in the high country. Check the listings below to see if you can legally bring your pet, and always indicate that you'll be camping with a pet when you make your reservation. See page 15 for the specifics about successfully arranging a campsite reservation.

There are also campground reservation offices at the Big Oak Flat Entrance (where Highway 120 enters the park from the west) and in Tuolumne Meadows (at the entrance to the campground). At times campsites can be arranged at the last minute by stopping at one of these offices. Call (209) 379-2123 for the Big Oak Flat and (209) 372-4025 for the Tuolumne Meadows office. The summer camping limit is 14 days outside of Yosemite Valley, and most of the campgrounds are open only in the summer. The limit extends to 30 days

the rest of the year, but be aware that you may only camp in Yosemite a total of 30 days in any one calendar year. For general park camping regulations, see page 95.

Hetch Hetchy Area Campgrounds

Crane Flat Campground

This camping area of 166 sites is situated at the 6,200-foot level, where Big Oak Flat Road and Tioga Road meet. Of all the campgrounds located outside Yosemite Valley, it's the closest—only 17 miles away. The nightly fee is $20, and reservations are required. Normally open from late June through early October, Crane Flat is close to the Merced and Tuolumne Big Tree groves and the Tioga Road attractions. Pets are allowed.

Hodgdon Meadow Campground

Here is the first place to camp when you enter Yosemite from the west on Highway 120 (you'll be 25 miles from Yosemite Valley). All types of campers are welcome in this campground consisting of 105 sites. To reach Hodgdon Meadow, turn down the hill just south of the Big Oak Flat Entrance. It's less than a half-mile to the campground entrance. Reservations are required between May and September ($20 per site); the rest of the year, it's a first-come, first-served facility ($14 per site). Pets are allowed.

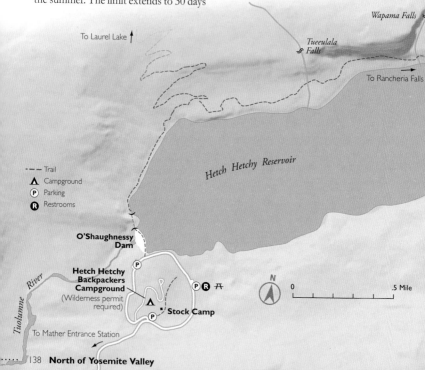

Wapama Falls

Tueeulala Falls

To Laurel Lake

To Rancheria Falls

Hetch Hetchy Reservoir

- – – Trail
▲ Campground
Ⓟ Parking
Ⓡ Restrooms

O'Shaughnessy Dam

Tuolumne River

Hetch Hetchy Backpackers Campground
(Wilderness permit required)

Stock Camp

To Mather Entrance Station

N

0   .5 Mile

Hetch Hetchy Backpackers Campground

This campground is exclusively for backpackers and other backcountry users (with wilderness permits) who are beginning their trips from the Hetch Hetchy trailhead. Stays are limited to one night at the beginning and end of wilderness outings. Located at Hetch Hetchy Reservoir, the campground features 19 backpacker sites (6 persons per site), 2 organized group sites (one accommodating 18 persons, the other 25), and 2 stock use sites (6 persons and 6 head of stock per site). Parking is provided near the campground, which has running water and flush toilets. No recreational vehicles, trailers, or pets are allowed. Prior arrangements should be made for the organized group and stock use sites. The fees are $5 per night for backpackers and $35 per site for the group and stock sites. Call (209) 372-0740.

Tioga Road Campgrounds

Tamarack Flat Campground

If you enjoy a more primitive camping experience (creek water that must be boiled and pit toilets), this campground fits the bill. It's located at 6,300 feet down a 3-mile dirt road that takes off Tioga Road about 4 miles east of Crane Flat (not suitable for large recreational vehicles or trailers). There are 52 campsites, the fee is $10 per night, and it's handled on a first-come, first-served basis. Usually open from late June through early October. No pets.

White Wolf Campground

A favorite of many high-country campers, White Wolf is set on a beautiful meadow alongside a bubbling creek. Added amenities are the White Wolf Lodge with a small store and restaurant, and public showers for a fee. The 8,000-foot setting 14 miles east of Crane Flat makes for cold nights and brilliant days. There are 74 first-come, first-served sites which rent for $14 per night (not suitable for RVs over 27 feet long). The camping season here is approximately July through September. Pets are allowed.

Yosemite Creek Campground

Another primitive campground, the Yosemite Creek camping area is located 5 miles down a narrow dirt road to the south of Tioga Road (the turnoff is less than a half-mile east of the White Wolf turnoff). Don't, repeat don't, even think about trying to take an RV or a trailer into this campground. The 75 sites utilize pit toilets and water from nearby Yosemite Creek (be sure to treat it). First-come, first-served, $10 per night, and open July through early September only. Pets are allowed.

Porcupine Flat Campground

They call it a flat campground, but there are flatter campgrounds in the world. There is no running water and no flush toilets here, but Porcupine Creek wanders by and the lodgepole pines make a fine canopy. Because the roads in the campground are very bad, recreational vehicles are limited to a few campsites at the entry to the campground; there are 52 sites total. The fee is $10 per night for these first-come, first-served sites. Open usually from July to October 15; no pets are allowed.

Tuolumne Meadows Campgrounds

Tuolumne Meadows Campground

Here is the park's largest single campground, with 304 sites. The road complex throughout the area is complicated and confusing, but once you get the hang of it, you'll love this campground. Families return here year after year for the camping, fishing, hiking, and scenery. Reservations are required for half the campsites, the balance are handled on a first-come, first-served basis. There's a store nearby, and a restaurant at Tuolumne Lodge, horseback riding at the stables, and fishing in the adjacent Tuolumne River. A sanitary dump station is also available. Backpackers and visitors without vehicles may take advantage of 25 walk-in sites for a fee of $5 per night, with a one-night maximum stay. Regular sites rent for $20 per night, and the camp is kept open from July through September in a typical year. Pets are allowed.

Tuolumne Group Campground

Special campsites within this campground are available for organized groups by prior arrangement. Reservations should be made in advance (see page 15). Each site, for tent camping only, can accommodate no fewer than 13 and no more than 30 people. No pets are allowed. For more information, call (209) 372-4025.

Gas

There are two Chevron gas stations in the north portion of Yosemite: one at Crane Flat and the other at Tuolumne Meadows. Only the Crane Flat station is open year-round. Major credit cards are accepted. If you are traveling Tioga Road, be sure to check your gas gauge, as it's a stretch of almost 40 miles where no services are provided. Check the *Yosemite Guide* for hours of operation.

A repair garage is open all year in Yosemite Valley, and towing service can be arranged 24 hours a day by calling (209) 372-8320.

Food: Restaurants

The north end of the park is relatively undeveloped. Visitors looking for fine restaurants and haute cuisine should try San Francisco or Los Angeles. While there are a few options for hearty meals in generally rustic facilities, you should plan on picnicking a lot and preparing your own food when you travel to Yosemite's north country. The following is a list of your choices (open only during the visitor season of July through September) should you choose to "dine out." Check the *Yosemite Guide* for dates and hours of operation.

Evergreen Lodge:

Not technically within the park, this old wooden lodge is 7 miles out Evergreen Road on the way to Hetch Hetchy. The simple dining room and unpretentious bar exude an unpolished charm, and the food is remarkably good. They serve dinner seven nights a week and breakfast on weekends (lunch items are available at the small store on the premises). The Evergreen Lodge is not listed in the *Yosemite Guide*, so call (209) 379-2606 for information on hours of operation and to make a reservation. Their normal season is from April through October. Moderate to expensive.

White Wolf Lodge

With its covered porch and its low-key, intimate dining room, the White Wolf Lodge, a whitewashed wooden structure, is an enjoyable spot to eat. Breakfast and dinner are served from a menu inside (grab a table on the porch if they're serving outdoors), and box lunches can be ordered and sandwiches and other items can be purchased from the adjacent store. There's a fine old fireplace, adequate food,

and beer and wine. When you consider that the staff gets spread pretty thin with their multiple duties, the service is fine. Dinner reservations are recommended; call (209) 372-8416. Moderate to expensive.

Tioga Pass Resort

Here's another spot that fails to qualify as a "park" establishment because it's two miles beyond the Tioga Pass Entrance on Forest Service land. But the place is a Yosemite institution and had to be included. They serve breakfast, lunch, and dinner in a room so small that many times you'll be asked to wait for long periods before you can be seated. The wait is worth it, however; try the homemade pies, delicious sandwiches, and substantial breakfasts. Get a load of the classic water spigot with rock-lined drain that's from some other era, and the wonderful curved counter. Recently they've added an outdoor coffee bar for those in quest of caffeine. For reservations, hours, or information, call (209) 372- 4471. Moderate prices.

Tuolumne Meadows Lodge

The dining room at the lodge is located in a canvas-sided tent-like structure that captures the feeling of roughing it in the high country. But the food will make you think you're someplace fancy. Breakfast and dinner are served from a menu family style; that is, you get seated with whoever happens to be present for mealtime when you are. It's good fun, and many fast friendships have been initiated in the lodge dining room. Beer and wine are served, and box lunches are available upon request. Dinner reservations are required and can be made by calling (209) 372-8413. Moderate to expensive prices.

Tuolumne Meadows Grill

Located adjacent to the Tuolumne store and post office, the grill is a great place for a hamburger. The service is as fast as you'll get anywhere, and they pour a big cup of coffee. Pull up a stool or stand and wolf. Fry-cooked meals are served at breakfast, lunch, and dinner (but the Lodge is preferred for breakfast if you're in no hurry). No reservations accepted (it's not that kind of place), and you can order menu items "to go." It also features delicious, cheap soft-serve ice cream. After a hike or a climb, nothing could be better. Inexpensive prices.

Food: Groceries

The following outlets are basic convenience stores with limited selections. Check the *Yosemite Guide* for operating hours.

Crane Flat Gas Station

Located in the main building of the Chevron station at the intersection of Big Oak Flat and Tioga Roads. Phone (209) 379-2742.

White Wolf Lodge

A very small camp store adjacent to the dining room at the lodge. Phone (209) 372-8416.

Tuolumne Meadows Store

This facility offers the largest selection and variety north of Yosemite Valley. Phone (209) 372-8428.

Lodging

As in the Wawona area, there are overnight accommodations in the north part of the park that are not operated by DNC Parks & Resorts at Yosemite. For reservations for DNC facilities, follow the steps outlined on page 14. You must deal directly with the other independent lodging providers to reserve with them. The quoted rates for the following listed lodging facilities are approximate and are subject to change.

Evergreen Lodge

Open April through October. Here are 18 rustic cabins on the road to Hetch Hetchy. Each cabin includes a private bath, but there are no kitchens. Other amenities are a restaurant, bar, and small convenience store. For reservations call directly to (800) 935-6343 or (209) 379- 2606. The web site address is www.evergreenlodge.com. Moderate to expensive.

White Wolf Lodge

Open in summer only. These rustic accommodations are situated at delightful White Wolf, bordered by meadow and forest both. There are four cabins with private bath (about $87) featuring propane heating, a desk, chair, dresser, and two double beds. Limited electricity is provided for lighting and heat. The 24 canvas tent cabins share a communal bathroom and shower house (about $67). The canvas cabins are equipped with beds with linens, candles for lighting, a wood-burning stove, and wood. There is no electricity. Special amenities include a dining

room and store. Reservations should be made through DNC (see page 14).

Tioga Pass Resort

Open Memorial Day through mid-October. Nestled on the side of a hill at well over the 9,000-foot level, the resort consists of 10 housekeeping cabins, 4 motel-type rooms, and a central building with restaurant, store, and gas pumps. A new addition is the outdoor coffee bar. It's two miles beyond Tioga Pass Entrance and just outside of the park. Weekly rates are offered. For reservations write PO Box 7, Lee Vining, CA 93541, or visit www.tiogapassresort.com. Moderate to expensive.

Tuolumne Meadows Lodge

Open in summer only. Here are 69 canvas tent cabins set close by the Tuolumne River in a picture-book setting. The tents are rustic and utilize wood stoves and candles (there's no electricity), but there are mattresses and linen on the beds. Bathrooms and showers are communal and anything but fancy. But that's part of the fun of the Tuolumne Lodge—it's roughing it easy. The tents rent for about $71 and will sleep up to 4. Reservations (which are much sought and highly coveted) should be made through DNC (see page 14).

View down Yosemite Valley to Half Dome from Tunnel View

7 | Getting to Yosemite

Most visitors to Yosemite arrive in private automobiles, but there are public transportation alternatives. Following are brief descriptions of those various alternatives, as well as detailed descriptions of the highway routes to Yosemite. If you need further information about transportation to Yosemite National Park, call (209) 372-0200 or visit http://www.nps.gov/yose/planyourvisit/publictransportation.htm.

By Air

Most people traveling to Yosemite by air fly into San Francisco, Oakland, or San Jose, roughly four hours from the park. The largest air terminal close to Yosemite served by a number of major airlines and several smaller ones is Fresno's. Formerly known as FAT (Fresno Air Terminal), the facility has been upgraded to the Fresno Yosemite International Airport (FYI). At this time there is no bus connection from the terminal to the park, and a rental car is required for the two-hour trip to Yosemite Valley. Rental cars are available from several major agencies in the terminal. A small airline also flies to Merced, and bus service to Yosemite is available from the Merced Airport on YARTS daily. Call (209) 388-9589 or (877) 989-2787 (the website is http://www.yarts.com). Rental cars also are available in Merced.

By Train

Train transportation is available to Yosemite from both Northern and Southern California. In Northern California, an Amtrak train originating in Emeryville carries passengers to Merced daily. Connection to Yosemite is made via the YARTS/Amtrak bus. For the return to Emeryville, an Amtrak train departs Merced daily.

From Southern California, Amtrak has trains departing from both Los Angeles and San Diego. The trip requires bus interconnects from Los Angeles to Bakersfield and from Merced to Yosemite. Return travelers can catch a YARTS/Amtrak bus to Merced for the Amtrak trip to Bakersfield and connections to Las Vegas and Southern California. For train and bus reservations call (800) USA-RAIL or visit http://www.amtrak.com/.

By Bus

For those staying in visitor accommodations surrounding the park, there is a car-free option: the Yosemite Area Regional Transportation System (YARTS) provides bus service from many of the communities outside Yosemite. Along the Highway 140 route, service is available from Merced, Catheys Valley, Mariposa, Midpines, and El Portal. From Highways 120 and 132, buses can be caught in Coulterville, Greeley Hill, Groveland, and Buck Meadows. Service also is available from Mammoth Lakes over Highway 120 during summer only. For information, call toll free to (877) 989-2787, or visit www.yarts.com.

By Automobile

There are four major routes to Yosemite National Park. Following is information on points of interest, restaurants, and motels along each route. The list is not meant to be exhaustive; rather, it reflects the preferences of the author. Because motels and restaurants are often short-lived, be sure to call ahead to avoid disappointment. All directions and orientations assume that one is traveling toward Yosemite.

Mileages to Yosemite Valley

Via Highway 41

From Los Angeles	313 miles
From Bakersfield	201 miles
From Fresno	94 miles
From Oakhurst	50 miles
From Fish Camp	37 miles

Via Highway 140

From Merced	81 miles
From Mariposa	43 miles
From El Portal	14 miles

Via Highway 120 from the West

From San Francisco	195 miles
From Sacramento	176 miles
From Stockton	127 miles
From Manteca	117 miles
From Oakdale	96 miles
From Groveland	49 miles

Via Highway 120 from the East

From Reno	218 miles
From Carson City	188 miles
From Bishop	146 miles
From Mammoth Lakes	106 miles
From Lee Vining	74 miles

Highway 41 from Fresno

Points of Interest

Located at 40637 Highway 41 in Oakhurst, across from Shilo Inn Suites as you head out of town, is the Oakhurst Visitor Center, a great place to get oriented, ask for directions, and find books and maps about Yosemite.

Fresno Flats Historical Park: Turn right at the second Oakhurst stoplight. Continue about half a mile to School Road (Road 427). Turn left and follow signs to this museum that includes a collection of old buildings depicting the lives of early settlers in the area. Hours are 1 to 3 p.m., Wednesday through Sunday.

Yosemite Mountain Sugar Pine Railroad, 56001 Highway 41 (one mile south of Fish Camp, on the right). Take time out for a ride on a historic logging train. Utilizing Shay steam locomotives and Model A–powered railcars, the railroad covers a four-mile loop. Many special events (including dinner trips) are offered throughout the year. A fee is charged for the ride. (559) 683-7273

Restaurants

Crab Cakes, 40278 Stagecoach Road, Oakhurst (on the left, just past the second stop light, behind Subway). Besides the namesake crab cakes, this small, well-run eatery serves fresh fish and shellfish, steak, chicken, and pasta. Meals include a bowl of delicious coleslaw and plenty of fresh bread. Patio seating is available. (559) 641-7667

Old Mexico Taqueria, 40083 Highway 41 (at the intersection of Highways 41 and 49), Oakhurst. This inexpensive outlet offers a lengthy menu of Mexican fare, and they prepare your choice as you wait in line. There are vegetarian options, and beer and wine are available. (559) 683-2777

Five Star Restaurant, 40484 Highway 41, Oakhurst (on the left, just south of the Best Western Motel). Very acceptable Chinese food that's right off the highway and right on the price. "Spicy" alternatives are available throughout the menu, and they will make your meal without MSG if you request it. (559) 641-5888.

Erna's Elderberry House and Bistro, Highway 41 and Victoria Lane, Oakhurst (on the left on the final descent into town). This is the proverbial diamond in the foothill rough. One of the few five-star rated restaurants in California, featuring old European cuisine with a California twist. Craig Claiborne of the *New York Times* spent three days here and wrote rave reviews. But beware, you must dress up and dinners are expensive. A less expensive alternative is Erna's wine cellar/bistro that serves simple but hearty dinners for about $15. (559) 683-6800

Oka Japanese Restaurant, 40291 Junction Drive, Oakhurst (turn left onto Highway 49, turn right at first stoplight). Despite the paintings of fish on the walls and other slightly odd bits of décor, this is a good place for sushi and features first-rate, generally authentic food. (559) 642-4850

Narrow Gauge Inn, 48571 Highway 41, Fish Camp (on the right just past the Yosemite Mountain Sugar Pine Railroad, one mile south of town). A rustic but charming dining room with an excellent menu. Open April to October only. (559) 683-6446

Sierra Restaurant (at Tenaya Lodge), 41122 Highway 41, Fish Camp (on the right as you enter town). Good selection of dishes including meat, seafood, salad, and sandwiches—all served by a cozy fireplace. The restaurant focuses on sustainable food sources and has several vegetarian options available. (559) 683-6555

Lodging

Oakhurst Lodge, 40302 Highway 41, Oakhurst (on the left just past Oakhurst's second stoplight). 60 units, inexpensive to moderate. (800) OK-LODGE (655-6343), or http://www.oklodge.com.

Shilo Inn, 40644 Highway 41, Oakhurst (on the left past the second stoplight). 80 mini-suite units, pool; inexpensive to moderate. (559) 683-3555, or http://www.shiloinns.com.

Yosemite Gateway Best Western, 40530 Highway 41, Oakhurst (on the left past the second stoplight). 122 units, indoor and outdoor pools and spas, restaurant; inexpensive to moderate. (559) 683-2378, or http://www.bestwestern.com.

Days Inn, 40662 Highway 41, Oakhurst (on the left past the second stoplight). 42 units, pool; inexpensive to moderate. (559) 642-2525, or http://www.daysinn.com.

Chateau du Sureau, Highway 41 and Victoria Lane, Oakhurst (on the left on the final descent into town). Affiliated with Erna's Elderberry House (see restaurants above), this is very expensive, luxury lodging. (559) 683-6860, or http://www.chateaudusureau.com.

Tenaya Lodge, 41122 Highway 41, Fish Camp (on the right as you enter Fish Camp). Indoor and outdoor pools, fitness center, cocktail lounge, restaurants; moderate to expensive. (559) 683-6555, or http://www.tenayalodge.com.

Narrow Gauge Inn, 48571 Highway 41, Fish Camp (on the right just past the Yosemite Mountain Sugar Pine Railroad, one mile south of Fish Camp). Pool; inexpensive to moderate. The motel is open all year. (559) 683-7720.

Highway 140 from Merced
Points of Interest
California State Mining and Mineral Museum, 5007 Fairgrounds Road, Mariposa (on the left side of Highway 49 at the Mariposa County Fairgrounds, about 1 mile south of town). A well-exhibited collection of minerals plus a mine tunnel and gold displays. An entrance fee is charged. (209) 742-7625.

Mariposa County Courthouse, 5088 Bullion Street, Mariposa (turn right on 8th Street near the middle of town, then left on Bullion). This handsome wooden building (erected in 1854) is the oldest courthouse in continuous use west of the Mississippi. Self-guided tours Monday through Friday: for more information, call the Mariposa County Visitors' Bureau at (209) 742-4567.

Mariposa History Center, 5116 Jesse Street, Mariposa (on the left side of Highway 140 towards the east end of town and next to the Bank of America). Historic displays and reconstructions of early-day Mariposa environments. Call for hours of operation. (209) 966-2924

Site of Savage's Trading Post, Highway 140, El Portal (on the right side of Highway 140, 22 miles east of Mariposa, at the confluence of the South and Main Forks of the Merced River). This is the actual site of an early-day trading post where Native Americans and miners went for supplies and goods. The gift shop specializes in Native American arts and crafts. You'll also find the trailhead for a hike up the South Fork of the Merced, which is ablaze with the colors of wildflowers in the spring. (209) 379-2301.

Yosemite Rail Exhibit, El Portal (turn left from Highway 140 onto El Portal Road and proceed one block to exhibit). Here are relics of early railroad activity in and around Yosemite, primarily old train cars and a locomotive. El Portal was the terminus of the Yosemite Valley Railroad.

Restaurants
Castillo's, 4995 Fifth Street, Mariposa (one block off Highway 140; turn right at The Vault). Castillo's is a good choice for regulation Mexican food. Outdoor seating available when weather permits. (209) 742-4413

Savoury's, 5034 Highway 140, Mariposa (on the left side in the historic block downtown). This small eatery has quickly become a favorite of the locals. The food is creative and excellent. Patio seating in summer. (209) 966-7677

Charles Street Dinner House, Highway 140 and Seventh Street, Mariposa (on the left, downtown). Good traditional food and plenty of it. A pretty sure bet. (209) 966-2366

Sugar Pine Café, 5038 Highway 140, Mariposa. A classic diner-style restaurant that serves breakfast and lunch only. Open Tuesdays through Sundays. A couple of vegetarian sandwich offerings round out a menu consisting of standards at reasonable prices. Peet's coffee is served. (209) 742-7793

Café at the Bug (Recovery Café and Bistro, at the Yosemite Bug Hostel), 6979 Highway 140, Midpines. The café serves inexpensive breakfasts and dinners, will pack "trail lunches," and serves beer and wine. A funky but cozy room filled with travelers gathering around the fireplace and well stocked with board games, this is an excellent spot to unwind. Wifi is available. This establishment is affiliated with the American Youth Hostel program. (209) 966-6666, or www.yosemitebug.com.

Lodging
Super 8 Motel, 5059 Highway 140, Mariposa (on the left about midway through town); inexpensive to moderate. (209) 966-4288, or http://www.super8.com.

Best Western Yosemite Way Station, 4999 Highway 140, Mariposa (on the left where Highway 140 intersects with Highway 49

South). Pool; inexpensive. (209) 966-7545, or http://www.bestwestern.com.

Mariposa Lodge, 5052 Highway 140, Mariposa (on the right about midway through town). Pool, pets are allowed; inexpensive. (209) 966-3607, or http://www.mariposalodge.com.

Mother Lode Lodge, 5051 Highway 140, Mariposa (on the left about midway through town). Pool, one kitchenette; inexpensive. (209) 966-2521, or http://www.mariposamotel.com.

Yosemite Bug Hostel, 6979 Highway 140, Midpines (on the left about two miles beyond "downtown" Midpines). This alternative group of accommodations includes dorm cabins, family and private rooms with both shared and private baths, tent cabins, and campsites. The hostel is very popular with backpacking travelers and enjoys an international clientele. Rates vary by the season, ranging from $16 plus tax for a dormitory bed to $115 plus tax for a private room. There are also a spa and restaurant on site. (209) 966-6666, (866) 826-7108, or http://www.yosemitebug.com.

Cedar Lodge, 9966 Highway 140, El Portal (on the right side of Highway 140). Pool, restaurant, bar; inexpensive to moderate. Operated by Yosemite Resorts: (888) 742-4371; outside the US call (209) 742-5282. Website is http://www.yosemiteresorts.us.

Yosemite Vacation Resort Homes, at Savage's Trading Post, El Portal. Extended-stay vacation homes and apartments, operated by Yosemite Resorts: (888) 742-4371; outside the US call (209) 742-5282. Website is http://www.yosemiteresorts.us.

Yosemite View Lodge, 11136 Highway 140, El Portal. On the right side of Highway 140 at the park boundary line. Gift shop, pools, restaurant; moderate to expensive. Operated by Yosemite Resorts: (888) 742-4371; outside the US call (209) 742-5282. Website is http://www.yosemiteresorts.us.

Highway 120 from Manteca

Points of Interest
Railtown 1897 State Historic Park, 11855 5th Avenue, Jamestown (just beyond town). This park features a 26-acre roundhouse-and-shop complex with steam locomotives and rolling passenger cars that have served the Sierra Railroad and Mother Lode since 1897. Open from 10 a.m. to 5 p.m. during summer and on

weekends in winter. (209) 984-4641

Downtown Jamestown. Main Street Jamestown is lined with shops, restaurants, and galleries housed in restored historic buildings. The gold rush theme predominates in this thriving tourist attraction.

Moccasin Creek Fish Hatchery, Moccasin (on the left side of Highway 49 about 100 feet south of its intersection with Highway 120). Take a self-guided tour of this facility operated by the California Department of Fish and Game, where one million catchable-size rainbow trout are produced annually for Sierra foothill reservoirs, streams, and rivers. Open 7:30 a.m. to 3 p.m. daily, year-round. (209) 989-2312.

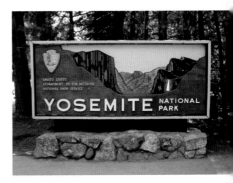

Big Oak Flat entrance, from Highway 120

Restaurants
National Hotel Restaurant and Gold Rush Saloon, 18183 Main Street, Jamestown (downtown). Serving California cuisine for lunch and dinner and brunch on Sundays. Their multi-page reasonably priced wine list highlights local Sierra foothills wine. Very friendly and attentive staff are eager to showcase the local bounty. Outdoor dining is available in summer. (209) 984-3902

Willow Steakhouse and Saloon, 18275 Main St. (at Willow), Jamestown. Dinner nightly, good for families. (209) 984-3998

Hotel Charlotte, 18736 Main St., Groveland (left side of Highway 120 in the center of town). They characterize their food as hearty California country cuisine. Open for dinner from April through October only. (209) 962-6455, or http://www.hotelcharlotte.com.

Groveland Hotel Restaurant, 18767 Main Street, Groveland (right side of Highway 120). Serving a varied menu prepared from California seasonal ingredients with herbs from the hotel's garden, and featuring an award-winning wine list. (209) 962-4000, or http://www.groveland.com.

Buck Meadows Restaurant, 7647 Highway 120, Buck Meadows (on the left where the road gets wide). Offering classic American cuisine, a variety of beer and wines, and daily specials. (209) 962-5281

Lodging

Groveland Hotel, 18767 Main Street, Groveland (right side of Highway 120). Rates for two are $135 to $210 (including breakfast). Midweek and winter specials are available. There is reputedly a ghost on the premises. Stay up late and you might see it. (209) 962-4000, or http://www.groveland.com.

Best Value Yosemite Westgate Lodge 7633 Highway 120, Buck Meadows. Inexpensive to moderate, depending on season. (209) 962-5281, or http://www.yosemitewestgate.com.

Highway 120 from Lee Vining

Lee Vining is at the intersection of Highways 120 and 395. A good website for the area is at http://www.monolake.org/chamber.

Points of Interest

Mono Lake County Park (5 miles north of Lee Vining on Highway 395). A great spot for a picnic, and there is outstanding bird watching here as well.

Mono Lake Committee Information Center and Bookstore, Highway 395, downtown Lee Vining. Operated by the Mono Lake Committee, the group primarily responsible for saving and restoring Mono Lake, this outlet offers free educational exhibits, slide shows, and movies to visitors, plus an excellent bookstore that also sells classy gifts. (760) 647-6386

Mono Lake Visitor Center, just north of Lee Vining on the right side of Highway 395. This impressive multi-agency facility is replete with modern displays, exhibits, a bookstore, slide shows, and a great deck overlooking the lake. For the story of Mono Lake, this is a must visit. An admission fee is charged.

Restaurants

Bodie Mike's Barbecue, Highway 395 and 4th St., Lee Vining. Featuring ribs, chicken, burgers, and a front patio. (760) 647-6432

Whoa Nellie Deli, intersection of Highways 120 and 395, Lee Vining. The place to be in the Eastern Sierra, this somewhat strange but absolutely wonderful establishment inside the Mobil Gas Mart features excellent food, including fish tacos, buffalo meatloaf, and lobster taquitos. You can even order a pitcher of margaritas. (760) 647-1088

Mono Lake

Tioga Pass Resort, Highway 120 (9 miles west of Lee Vining). A local landmark, famous for its homemade pies (see page 140). (209) 372-4471, or http://www.tiogapassresort.com.

Lodging

El Mono Motel and Latte Da Coffee Café, Highway 395 at 3rd St., Lee Vining. This sweet, spiffed-up motel is attached to a funky coffee shop where organic coffee is served. It's a favorite of locals, and you'll feel like you're one of the family there. Excellent service and reasonable prices. (760) 647-6310, or http://www.elmonomotel.com.

Best Western Lake View Lodge, 51285 Highway 395, Lee Vining. A nice motel run by even nicer people; inexpensive. (760) 647-6543, or (800) 528-1234, or http://www.bwlakeviewlodge.com.

Murphey's Motel, Highway 395, Lee Vining. A decent motel with a AAA rating. One of the buildings is rustic, the other contemporary; inexpensive, and they give discounts to ice climbers. (760) 647-6316, or http://www.murpheysyosemite.com.

Tioga Pass Resort, Highway 120, 9 miles west of Lee Vining. The resort is famous for backcountry ski access and pie. 10 housekeeping cabins and 4 motel-type units; inexpensive to moderate. (209) 372-4471, or http://www.tiogapassresort.com.

Yosemite on the Internet

There are lots of online resources available about Yosemite. Whether found on sites maintained by the government or on the personal pages of passionate Yosemite lovers, information, photographs, maps, and stories are abundant. Here are some of the best available at this time.

Yosemite National Park Home Page

http://www.nps.gov/yose

This is the official park website, maintained by the National Park Service. Here you will find lots of visitor information, nuts and bolts data, the latest weather conditions, government news releases, a section about park planning and management issues, programs for students, podcasts, and a park map. Also available online are a series of interesting videos on topics such as fire ecology, birding, and bears.

Yosemite Conservancy

http://www.yosemiteconservancy.org

This full-featured site is known for its webcam views of Yosemite Valley, its information about visitor programs, its extensive news archives, a variety of diary accounts about Yosemite, and an area dedicated to natural history issues in the Sierra. There's also an extensive online Yosemite Store.

DNC Parks & Resorts at Yosemite

http://www.yosemitepark.com

Operated by the park's chief concessioner, this site is most important for the information it provides about lodging options in Yosemite, including online reservations. There's also information about special events, discount offers, and jobs in the park.

Recreation.gov

http://www.recreation.gov

This site provides an easy and convenient way to make camping reservations (using a credit card) for Yosemite and other national park campgrounds. It certainly beats trying to use their phone-in system. Options are available for individual, family, and group sites at all campgrounds that require reservations (see page 15).

NatureBridge

http://www.naturebridge.org/yosemite

This organization offers environmental education in the park, and their site offers a program orientation slide show, information about the educational curriculum, organizational data, and teacher resources. For school groups interested in a high-quality learning experience in Yosemite, this is the place to check.

The Yosemite Conservancy Bookstore

http://www.yosemiteconservancystore.com

For visitors wanting information, books, maps, gifts, and other Yosemite-related products, this site is made to order. The collection of items available is extensive, all products are illustrated in color, and the ordering process (with a credit card) is efficiently handled through a secure server. Yosemite Conservancy members can take advantage of a 15% discount on most purchases, too.

Yosemite Guide Online

http://www.nps.gov/yose/planyourvisit/guide.htm

This site allows prospective visitors to download the *Yosemite Guide* in a PDF version. The *Yosemite Guide* contains a calendar of guided programs and park activities, as well as hours of operation for visitor centers and museums.

Photo Credits

Cover: Yosemite Falls, by Jeff Grandy

1: Fall color at Yosemite © Artifan 2011, used under license from Shutterstock.com

2: Half Dome © Chee-Onn Leong 2011, used under license from Shutterstock.com

3: Hike in Yosemite mountains © Galyna Andrushko 2011, used under license from Shutterstock.com

5: Marmot © Heather L. Jones 2011, used under license from Shutterstock.com

6: Young hiker © Teri and Jackie Soares 2011, used under license from Shutterstock.com

7: Dogwood © Steven Castro 2011, used under license from Shutterstock.com

1: Welcome to Yosemite

8–9: Half Dome at twilight from Glacier Point © Dean Pennala 2011, used under license from Shutterstock.com

14: Curry Village, courtesy of DNC Parks & Resorts at Yosemite

15: Happy camper © Kokhanchikov 2011, used under license from Shutterstock.com

17: Hiker in Yosemite © Galyna Andrushko 2011, used under license from Shutterstock.com

18: Hiking near May Lake © Tom Grundy 2011, used under license from Shutterstock.com

19: Black bear cub © Holly Kuchera 2011, used under license from Shutterstock.com

20: View from Glacier Point © Kara Jade Quan-Montgomery 2011, used under license from Shutterstock.com

21: Ranger on a horse, courtesy of the Yosemite NPS Archive

22: Bridalveil Fall in winter, photograph by Christine Loberg, courtesy of the artist

23: Winter in Wawona, courtesy of the Yosemite NPS Archive

24: Outdoor dining at the Ahwahnee, © Steve Broer 2011, used under license from Shutterstock.com

25: A picnic in the valley, © James Steidl 2011, used under license from Shutterstock.com

25: Golden-mantled ground squirrel, © kenkistler 2011, used under license from Shutterstock.com

27: Yosemite Falls © CaptureLight 2011, used under license from Shutterstock.com

28: View of Yosemite Valley from Glacier Point © JaredWCarter 2011, used under license from Shutterstock.com

29: Climbers on Lost Arrow Spire © Greg Epperson 2011, used under license from Shutterstock.com

30: Climbing Yosemite, off of Daff © Tom Grundy 2011, used under license from Shutterstock.com

31: Climbing a sheer rock face © Greg Epperson 2011, used under license from Shutterstock.com

31: Climbing El Capitan © Marc Pagani Photography 2010, used under license from Shutterstock.com

32: Wawona Visitor Center, photograph by Josh Helling, courtesy of Yosemite Conservancy

2: Yosemite History

34–35: Early tourists in the valley, courtesy of the Yosemite NPS Library

36: Native American family, courtesy of Yosemite NPS Library

37: Native American basket, courtesy of Yosemite NPS Library

38: Yosemite Falls by Thomas Ayres, courtesy of the Yosemite NPS Library

39: Clark's Station, courtesy of the Yosemite NPS Library

39: Early tourists, courtesy of the Yosemite NPS Library

40: Troop F on the Fallen Monarch tree, courtesy of the Yosemite NPS Library

41: Buffalo Soldiers, 24th Mounted Infantry, courtesy of the Yosemite NPS Library

42: John Muir and Theodore Roosevelt, courtesy of the Yosemite NPS Library

43: Historic Wells Fargo Office at Pioneer Yosemite History Center, courtesy of the Yosemite NPS Archive

44: Nature walk, courtesy of the Yosemite NPS Library

45: El Capitan meadow © Steven Castro 2011, used under license from Shutterstock.com

46: Yosemite Chapel © EastVillage Images 2011, used under license from Shutterstock.com

50: Galen Clark, courtesy of the Yosemite NPS Library

51: James Mason Hutchings, courtesy of the Yosemite NPS Library

51: John Muir, courtesy of the Yosemite NPS Library

52: David Curry, courtesy of the Yosemite NPS Library

52: Jenny Curry, courtesy of the Yosemite NPS Library

52: Ansel Adams, courtesy of the Yosemite NPS Library

54: Lembert Dome © Kara-Jade Quon Montgomery 2011, used under license from Shutterstock.com

55: Tuolumne Meadows from Tioga Road © Israel Pabon 2011, used under license from Shutterstock.com

3: Yosemite's Natural World

56: Great gray owl © Kaido Karner 2011, used under license from Shutterstock.com

58: Glacial erratics at Olmsted Point © pixy 2011, used under license from Shutterstock.com

59: Yosemite Valley © Andy Z. 2011, used under license from Shutterstock.com

60: View of Half Dome from Olmsted Point© Kara Jade Quan-Montgomery 2011, used under license from Shutterstock.com

61: Upper and Lower Yosemite Falls © EastVillage Images 2011, used under license from Shutterstock.com

63: Burned trees at Smith Peak © Nickolay Stanev 2011, used under license from Shutterstock.com

64: A flooded meadow © Sasha Buzko 2011, used under license from Shutterstock.com

65: Autumn Merced River reflection © Steven Castro 2011, used under license from Shutterstock.com

65: Ponderosa pine cones on the forest floor © Brian Balster 2011, used under license from Shutterstock.com

66: Alpine lily, western azalea, sneezeweed, fleabane daisy, wandering daisy, Lewis's monkeyflower, Mariposa lily, western monkshood, pussypaws, scarlet gilia, snow plant, Sierra stickseed by Eric Schaal, courtesy of the artist

67: Sequoia © urosr 2011, used under license from Shutterstock.com

68: Black bear © Lana Langlois 2011, used under license from Shutterstock.com

69: Mule deer © Michael Klenetsky 2011, used under license from Shutterstock.com

70: Pika © Jean-Francois Rivard 2011, used under license from Shutterstock.com

71: Mountain lion © visceralimage 2011, used under license from Shutterstock.com

72: Coyote © Julie Lubick 2011, used under license from Shutterstock.com

72: Chipmunk © Michael Woodruff 2011, used under license from Shutterstock.com

73: Marmot on top of Half Dome © Mark Yarchoan 2011, used under license from Shutterstock.com

73: Bighorn sheep © visceralimage 2011, used under license from Shutterstock.com

74: Acorn woodpecker © Stubblefield Photography 2011, used under license from Shutterstock.com

74: American dipper © IPK Photography 2011, used under license from Shutterstock.com

74: Clark's nutcracker © Steve Bower 2011, used under license from Shutterstock.com

74: Black-headed grosbeak © teekaygee 2011, used under license from Shutterstock.com

75: Great horned owl © artcphotos 2011, used under license from Shutterstock.com

75: Peregrine falcon © Four Oaks 2011, used under license from Shutterstock.com

76: Pacific tree frog © David Gn 2011, used under license from Shutterstock.com

76: Western fence lizard © Steve Byland 2011, used under license from Shutterstock.com

77: Brook trout © Tom Grundy 2011, used under license from Shutterstock.com

77: Rainbow trout © Wesley Aston 2011, used under license from Shutterstock.com

78: Rattlesnake © Stephen Mcsweeny 2011, used under license from Shutterstock.com

79: Poison oak © Jerry-Rainey 2011, used under license from Shutterstock.com

79: Black widow © URRRA 2011, used under license from Shutterstock.com

80: Peregrine falcon © Sue Robinson 2011, used under license from Shutterstock.com

80: Bighorn sheep © visceralimage 2011, used under license from Shutterstock.com

81: Sierra Nevada yellow-legged frog by Rick Kuyper, courtesy of USF&W Service

81: Bald eagle © Kane 513 2011, used under license from Shutterstock.com

82: Willow flycatcher © Steve Byland 2011, used under license from Shutterstock.com

4: Yosemite Valley

82–83: El Capitan and the Merced River © Katrina Leigh 2011, used under license from Shutterstock.com

86: Yosemite Visitor Center, courtesy of the Yosemite NPS Archive

88: Lee Stetson as John Muir, courtesy of Lee Terkelsen

88: Vernal Fall and the Mist Trail © Thomas Siggia 2011, used under license from Shutterstock.com

90: Rafting the Merced River © May-skyphoto 2011, used under license from Shutterstock.com

91: Ranger Shelton Johnson, courtesy of the Yosemite NPS Archive

92: Mirror Lake © Chee-Onn Leong 2011, used under license from Shutterstock.com

93: Lower Yosemite Fall © Kenneth Rush 2011, used under license from Shutterstock.com

94: Climbing Half Dome © Jason Maehl 2011, used under license from Shutterstock.com

94: Half Dome from the northeast © Andrew McDonough 2011, used under license from Shutterstock.com

95: Camping at nightfall © Galyna Andrushko 2011, used under license from Shutterstock.com

98: Camp Curry © Eoghan McNally 2011, used under license from Shutterstock.com

99: The Ahwahnee Hotel, courtesy of DNC Parks & Resorts at Yosemite

5: South of Yosemite Valley

102–103: Dogwood blossoms, photograph by Christine Loberg, courtesy of the artist

106: The Mariposa Grove Museum © Jarno Gonzalez Zarraonandia 2010, used under license from Shutterstock.com

108: Cavalry at Camp A. E. Wood, courtesy of Yosemite NPS Library

109: Stagecoach exiting covered bridge, photograph by Josh Helling, courtesy of Yosemite Conservancy

110: Top of Chilnualna Fall © Mordy Neuman 2011, used under license from Shutterstock.com

110: Ranger Burl Maier driving stagecoach, photograph by Josh Helling, courtesy of Yosemite Conservancy

111: Mules © Jorg Hackemann 2011, used under license from Shutterstock.com

114: The Bachelor and Three Graces © Christophe Testi 2011, used under license from Shutterstock.com

116: View from Sentinel Dome © Rick Parsons 2011, used under license from Shutterstock.com

117: Camping in the forest © Sahani Photography 2011, used under license from Shutterstock.com

118: Wawona Hotel, photograph by Christine Loberg, courtesy of the artist

119: Wawona Golf Course © Carol Afshar 2011, used under license from Shutterstock.com

6: North of Yosemite Valley

120–121: Tuolumne Meadows Landscape © Dean Pennala 2011, used under license from Shutterstock.com

124: Tenaya Lake © Junne 2011, used under license from Shutterstock.com

124: White Cascade, Glen Aulin High Sierra Camp © Rick Whitacre 2011, used under license from Shutterstock.com

125: O'Shaughnessy Dam © Christophe Testi 2010, used under license from Shutterstock.com

126: Hetch Hetchy Reservoir © Nickolay Stanev 2011, used under license from Shutterstock.com

128: Gaylor Lakes © Steve Kuhn Photography 2011, used under license from Shutterstock.com

129: View from Olmsted Point © Eugene Moerman 2011, used under license from Shutterstock.com

133: Tuolumne Meadows © Doug Lemke 2011, used under license from Shutterstock.com

134: Hikers on Lembert Dome © Steve Kuhn Photography 2011, used under license from Shutterstock.com

135: Dog Lake © JaredWCarter 2011, used under license from Shutterstock.com

136: Cathedral Lake © Rick Whitacre 2011, used under license from Shuttertock.com

136: Soda Springs © ArnaudS2 2011, used under license from Shutterstock.com

137: Early morning rainbow © Rick Whitacre 2011, used under license from Shutterstock.com

7: Getting to Yosemite

142–143: View down Yosemite Valley © Steve Heap 2011, used under license from Shutterstock.com

147: Big Oak Flat entrance © William Silver 2011, used under license from Shutterstock.com

148: Mono Lake © Tung Tran 2011, used under license from Shutterstock.com

156: Mist in the valley © Jeffrey Kreulen 2011, used under license from Shutterstock.com

157: Steve Medley, courtesy of the Medley family

158: View from Tioga Pass © kavram 2011, used under license from Shutterstock.com

Index

Mist in the valley

 **Author Steve Medley,** hiker, president of the Yosemite Association, and constant friend of the park, died in the fall of 2006. He spent 35 of his 57 years in Yosemite National Park, starting out as a ranger before moving to the Yosemite Association, which he led for over two decades. He was one of Yosemite's greatest supporters, building the Yosemite Association into a tremendous force on behalf of the park and leaving a legacy of educational publications for park visitors to enjoy. Beyond his professional duties, his love for Yosemite was founded on and renewed by lengthy trips into the deepest backcountry. A map of routes he hiked looks a lot like a map of Yosemite's trail network. His energy, drive, and great good humor made him as beloved around Yosemite as Yosemite was to him. He is greatly missed.

Play a part in protecting Yosemite.
Together we can make a difference.

Yosemite Conservancy is the only philanthropic organization dedicated exclusively to preserving and protecting Yosemite and enriching the visitor experience.

OUR WORK IS EVERYWHERE

We are in the park year-round. Many of the trails you hike, wildlife you see or magnificent overlooks that you visit are here because of our work and your support. We provide visitor programs like Outdoor Adventures, theater and art classes. Every summer our volunteers work on projects in habitat restoration, or provide visitor information throughout the park.

THRIVING HABITAT AND HAPPY VISITORS

Yosemite Conservancy funds work that protects meadows, lake areas and other fragile habitats while giving visitors better access to a wilderness experience. We do this by supporting miles of trail restoration, and the installation of ecologically friendly universal-access paths—great for both visitors and the environment.

EDUCATING THE NEXT GENERATION OF STEWARDS

Every year, Yosemite Conservancy funds programs that offer hundreds of youth the chance to participate in courses that combine the best in youth development with park preservation. These educational courses put youth on paths to college, park internships or employment.

YOUR SUPPORT MAKES A DIFFERENCE

By supporting the Conservancy, you join a community that is committed to protecting Yosemite for future generations.

As a "thank you" for your gift of $25 or more you will receive:

- Special "Passport" with offers and discounts for use in and around the park
- 15 percent discount on books, maps and many items sold by Yosemite Conservancy stores in the park and online
- 15 percent discount on outdoor adventures conducted by the Conservancy in Yosemite
- Listing in the Honor Register at the Valley Visitor Center in Yosemite
- Subscription to our magazine

HOW TO GIVE

Visit: yosemiteconservancy.org
Call: 1-800-469-7275
Email: info@yosemiteconservancy.org

LET US CONNECT YOU TO YOSEMITE

Find out more about our year-round programs and explore everything Yosemite has to offer.

Want to hike Half Dome with an expert guide?

Need a fun family camping trip where you don't have to cook?

Would you like to learn painting or photography in a stunning setting?

Want to catch a theatre performance during the summer?

Visit yosemiteconservancy.org for the latest program information, or call 1-800-469-7275.

Or stop by one of our bookstores while you're in the park. Proceeds from purchases benefit essential projects in the park.

YOSEMITE
CONSERVANCY.

Notes